GO FOR THE GREEN

GO FOR THE GREEN

by

Garry Hoyt

iUniverse, Inc.
New York Bloomington

Go For The Green
The New Case for Sail and Solar Power

iUniverse books may be ordered through booksellers or by contacting:

iUniverse
1663 Liberty Drive
Bloomington, IN 47403
www.iuniverse.com
1-800-Authors (1-800-288-4677)

Because of the dynamic nature of the Internet, any Web addresses or links contained in this book may have changed since publication and may no longer be valid. The views expressed in this work are solely those of the author and do not necessarily reflect the views of the publisher, and the publisher hereby disclaims any responsibility for them.

ISBN: 978-1-4401-4809-5 (pbk)
ISBN: 978-1-4401-4811-8 (dj)
ISBN: 978-1-4401-4810-1 (ebk)

Library of Congress Control Number: 2009931973

Printed in the United States of America

iUniverse rev. date: 9/17/2009

Contents

GO with the WiNd

In order to begin with a compact review, on the opposite page I have attempted to artistically compress the spectrum of small boat sailing into a single page sketch. It is not accidental that most of the boats shown are single handers, because I believe that single handing is the best sailing skill, as well as the key to sailing's deserved greater popularity. To emphasize utilitarian roots, the workboat American Cat is placed at the center, bordered by the sloop, kite sailer, foiling moth, multihull, windsurfer and planing dinghy that have emerged as blossoms. Who knows what further innovations are yet to be discovered, all within the pleasing parameters of natural, non-polluting wind power?

I charge future generations with the responsibility of imaginatively fulfilling sailing's heritage as the original medium of discovery.

Garry Hoyt

Part I
New Considerations

"Go For The Green"

The New Case For Sail and Solar Power

Introduction

This book has three interlocking missions. The first is to make you a better sailor, which I shall endeavor to accomplish by enlisting and compacting sixty five years of experience on the water. The second is to explore ways to make sailing a more widely accepted and enjoyed practice, in effect, reversing a disquieting ten year decline in the sport. And the third is to relate the needed growth in sailing to the greater cause of environmental concerns, and to suggest a new alliance between sail and solar electric power. To advance these three interlocking missions, the book is divided into two parts. Part I, *New Considerations*, begins with an historical review of where sailing has been and then delves into new directions for sailing to go. Part II, *Design Solutions*, is devoted to describing new design concepts and includes specific illustrations of new rigs and how they might work on different hull configurations.

My starting premise is the prediction that ten years from now, the recreational use of carbon based fuels on the water will be accorded the same level of social scorn and rejection that smoking now receives. Those doubting that prediction should recall that thirty years ago smoking was a widely popular, heavily promoted and socially esteemed practice. Now smoking is medically condemned and legally restricted, as a dangerous intrusion on everyone's basic right to fresh air. Similarly, in the near future the notion that anybody has a recreational right to shatter the restorative silence that should be everybody's basic right on the water, while simultaneously polluting the surrounding air and water, contributing to the danger of global warming and in the process sending billions of dollars to finance the enemies that hate us most, all in the name of nautical amusement, this will increasingly be seen as an unacceptable strategy of stunning stupidity and terminal short sightedness.

Just as hard evidence on the dangers of second hand smoke escalated smoking from a personal nuisance to a public menace, so now the clear link between fossil fuels and global warming has created an imperative to actively reduce and eventually replace the recreational marine use of gasoline and diesel engines. Obviously, this same indictment should extend equally to snowmobiles and the flagrant environmental abuse of NASCAR racing, but that is beyond the scope of this book. This is a specific notice to mariners. As the original property owners in this area, sailors should unite with canoeists, kayakers and rowers to form a National constituency to serve as the vanguard for protective action.

None of the above should be confused with some idealistic, unrealistic, tree hugging environmental zealotry. It is simply an old sailor's eye trained to look to the horizon for wind shifts and impending weather. The point here is that the predictable and necessary disqualification of carbon based fuel for marine recreation should set the stage and drive new ingenuity in the harnessing of sail and solar electric power as new alternatives for water based recreation.

For early on reporting of the impact of marine fuel on the environment, credit is due to author Andre Mele, whose prescient book, "Polluting for Pleasure" was a wake up call to the problem in 1993. Unfortunately nobody, including me, paid proper attention. But the passing years have added the weight of accumulated evidence to Mele's warnings, and the fears of global warming that were dismissed back then as liberal hysteria, have proven all too true today. So let's not repeat that error by being afraid to actively challenge the present pattern of powerboat design, which must drastically move away from fossil fuel dependence.

Let's admit at the outset that it is not presently possible and it may never be possible for sail power to be as fast and easy as engine power. But the overarching reality it that we must make the shift away from the present reliance on fossil fueled engines. One accepts that reliance as a current necessity for commercial fishermen, general marine transportation, Navy, Coast Guard and military use, and in those areas it will take time to make the shift away. So the best place to start the necessary correction is in the recreational area, where engine power is a *convenience* not a necessity. There is no sense pretending that sail by itself is the answer for everybody, and that is where solar electric power comes in as a natural partner and a new means for re-directing powerboat interest to greener solutions.

It bears repeating, that global warming may be the central problem of our time and the biggest single contributor to global warming is emissions from fossil fuels. Therefore, the only responsible conclusion is that the recreational use of fossil fuel must be stringently reduced and eventually terminated because it is not environmentally conscionable. That is the tough but accurate assessment that must impel action.

Of course it is possible, as many claim, that all these fears of global warming are vastly exaggerated and what changes we see are simply a matter of natural cycles. Let me say that I sincerely hope they are right, but I fear they are not and the cautious mariner must always plan for the worst.

Go For The Gold was a book written by me, and published in 1971 by Vanguard, then a division of The New York Times. It dealt with the development of sailboat racing skills, and was well received at the time. Gary Jobson later told me that every member of the successful America' Cup team on *Courageous* had read the book and sailors in general were kind with their comments. It was interesting to see how my title phrase Go For The Gold took hold and eventually became common jargon for sports casters. I deliberately say "my phrase" because I had taken considerable thought to come up with the phrase, which was copyrighted in my name. But perhaps the best evidence of originality came in the vigorous objection of the publisher and editors at Vanguard. "What does this mean?" they asked "Are you talking about some sort of treasure hunt?" "Nobody will understand" was their persistent critique. However, I stubbornly resisted their requests for a title change, and so *Go For The Gold* began its career from the title of a small book about a minor sport to a now widely accepted standard exhortation for competitive sports excellence.

Go For The Green obviously trades on that now-familiar acceptance, and given the current commercial clamor of companies claiming "green" credentials, I trust the environmental implications are clear. My real point in bringing all this up is simply to lay prideful claim to *Go For The Gold* as a phrase I originated 40 years ago and to hope that

Go For The Green might be a similar rallying call to all who love the sea to reclaim the fragile magic that has engaged mariners throughout the years. To leave a lesser legacy to following generations would amount to selfish dereliction of duty and penurious underpayment for pleasures received.

Garry Hoyt

Chapter 1—The Evolving Fortunes of Sail Power

This is not a detailed history, but rather a conceptual review of where Sail has been with an eye to where it needs to go in the future. Technical points will be made in non-technical terms.

For perspective, it is important to recognize that for roughly three thousand years, sailing represented the preeminent technology of its day. Because sailing was the exclusive means of distance travel, trade, exploration, and military power. There is probably no other technology that matches sailing's sustained impact on the course of history and the spread of civilization. Sail ranks right up there with the wheel as a vital link in human progress because sail was literally the prime medium of discovery that opened up the modern world.

This then is a legacy of serious importance, and it is instructive to follow how sail technology has progressed and also how it has been slowed and distracted. Persistent market decline, particularly in the U.S., needs to be addressed. Here it is necessary to note that sailing technology cannot realistically be separated from sailing commerce because the two are highly interdependent. And so when markets fail or falter, it is often because technology has not fully kept pace with new circumstances and new competitive alternatives.

When we talk of sailing it is also important to separate sail from other more frivolous recreational diversions such as golf, or tennis, or bowling or basketball or baseball. All of these are artificial activities devised purely for amusement or exercise, they have no practical roots, nor do they aspire to any. Sailing, in contrast, is a very natural endeavor that sprang directly from practical need. From the earliest days man needed to get across large bodies of water as rapidly and reliably as possible for the business of fishing, of commerce, or warfare or exploration or carrying people and news.

Speculating about origins, one can reasonably suppose that wood's inherent power of flotation and the ability of flotation to lessen the carrying load, was easily and early observed. Lacking was something to add propulsion and mobility to flotation. Sail emerged as the best, indeed the only means to accomplish this, because it combined an abundant, free source of power, the wind, with an ability to function with a variety of the crudest shapes made with the simplest materials.

Thus the early cave man, seated astride a floating log, discovered that by spreading an animal skin, he could be blown in the direction of the wind, with more speed and less effort than by paddling. We can also imagine that these early cave man sailors rather quickly tired of the frequent tip overs that were the inevitable price of spreading sail atop a rolly log. A log is the prime example of a hull form with no *form stability*. Form stability is the stability that is derived from the shape of the hull, as opposed to stability derived from the weight of ballast. Resolving this issue of stability was an early on sail problem, and remains so today.

By way of solution, these early sailors figured out that lashing together two or three logs made a crude but stable raft that could carry more people, or a slain deer or whatever. Of course carrying more weight sank the log raft lower in the water, which increased the drag of wetted surface, which made the raft slower and quickly established the need for more sail power. And so they had to spread more animal skins to the wind via supporting sticks. And since holding up sticks with skins was hard hand work, they figured out how to tie vines to the sticks to hold them in place, and so rigging was born.

Of course crude log rafts with crude skin sails could really only go dead downwind, which was not necessarily where you wanted or needed to go. So somebody got smart, stuck a paddle vertically between the logs and discovered that by creating *lateral resistance*, the raft could be made to sail at right angles to the wind with reduced slipping sideways. That opened up another 180º of the compass. Not perfect, but markedly better than the hard work of constant paddling.

The critical, remaining problem was how to go *against the wind*, a move that defies logic. When you can take a strong natural force that's blowing against you and convert it to a drive force pushing you forward the other way, that's pretty neat, sort of like defying gravity. That's was sailing does quietly, naturally, with no cost and no pollution, a considerable feat that sets sailing apart from any other form of propulsion.

It can be seen that right from the very start that all the basic problems of sailing had to be faced and to some degree solved. These problems still exist for the most sophisticated designs of today, and they can be summarized as follows:

1. Provide sufficient sail power to create the drive force forward.

2. Provide sufficient stability (righting moment) to carry the sail power without tipping over.

3. Provide enough lateral resistance to keep from sliding sideways.

4. Minimize the burden of weight.

5. Minimize the drag of wetted surface.

You have only to comprehend these factors and you will have a grasp of the basic issues facing sailboat designers. Solve these problems better and you will have a better design. Understand them better and you will be a better sailor. And these solutions are not limited to trained engineers. Some of the best ideas in sailing have come from people with no previous training in sailboat design. There can even be some advantage to technical inexperience in that when you have no command of the complexities, you are forced into simplicities. Extensive technical knowledge can tempt the designer into arcane solutions that the sea has no tolerance for. As will be repeated in this book, *simplicity is the ultimate sophistication.*

Beyond its direct transportation utility, sail power, again right from the start, was a stern instructor in the consequentiality of things. Long before such concepts were fashionable, sail power at sea was an equal opportunity destroyer. It didn't matter whether you were white or black, male or female, old or young, noble or peasant, a mistake at sea meant down you went. The ocean is relentlessly even handed in its dispersed distribution of danger and sailors were repeatedly taught that there is nothing that man makes that the sea in its marshaled fury cannot break. As a result, sailors were obliged to acquire a cautious and disciplined behavior for survival. Yet they had to be willing to daringly cross those lines of restraint when opportunity beckoned. Thus, the lessons of risk and reward were early taught in sailing ships at sea because every voyage involved certain risk for uncertain results. Early sea captains were pioneer venture capitalists, but in contrast to the modern variety, there was no government bail out handy and their lives were often part of the high price of failure. And predatory pirates like Madoff didn't make bail or jail, they made the yard arms.

So it was that for centuries, prowess in sail power virtually dictated a nation's rate of success in commerce, warfare and the critical ability to find and control new lands. And naturally, the best minds of those times concentrated their ingenuity on designing and building sailing ships that could carry more men, more goods, more guns, with the ability to sail ever closer to the wind. For centuries, information and ideas literally moved at the speed of sail. This preeminence of sail assured a constant press for innovation, and progress was steady and occasionally dramatic.

Not every nation did this equally well, and their relative success or failure in sail power was directly reflected in their commercial, military and national power. Britain did it best for longest and by virtue of the naval superiority that derived directly from better sail power, that small island nation became the largest empire in the world. Being able to design, build and man superior sailing ships gave the British a naval edge that was the equivalent of a nuclear power edge in today's world. Because control of the sea ways meant control of the communications and supplies upon which military success was totally dependent. That the American colonies were able to succeed against this overwhelming power makes the story of the American Revolution all the more remarkable.

And for the emerging, independent American colonies, prowess in sail power was an early marker of the nation's potential. America led the world in the then important whaling industry and the American Clipper Ships represented the zenith of ship building skill—very daring and leading edge in its day. And progress in sail power was continuous as long as sail had dominant, commercial and military value.

But with the advent of steam power, sail abruptly lost its exclusive commercial and military value, and technological attention quickly turned elsewhere. Sailing drifted into the backwaters and eddies of a rich man's sport, and precipitously descended from primary transportation for everybody to recreational diversion for a few. What little design urgency remained was focused on racing, and racing quickly developed rules, mostly in the form of exclusions and complications often designed primarily to keep the game intact and comprehensible only to those already playing it. A sense of "newcomers need not apply" seemed to prevail. Sailing speed became important only in the relative sense—that is speed relative to other boats limited by the same rules. Rules are directly detrimental to innovation, and so sailing, which had previously invited and rewarded innovation, began to resist it and even outlaw it. These tendencies were a sure fire formula for shrinkage and stagnation.

A good illustration of this came when Nathaniel Herreshoff, the preeminent American designer produced the catamaran *Amaryllis* back in 1876 and soundly thrashed all the best monohulls in an important New York regatta. For this impertinence in daring to sail faster, Amaryllis and all multihulls were banished from the race course by the powers that were, an exile from which multihulls only recently began to recover. That's over one hundred years in the doghouse for the high crime of higher speed. It's hard to see how banning better speed in any way serves the cause of sailing. Yet much of the effort and structure of sailing organizations seems contrived to resist or inhibit speed improvements.

For example, One Design racing is a bedrock of sailing activity, and it remains both an enjoyable practice and the best way to develop good sailors. But the popularity of One Design racing is a contradiction of design progress because it specifically freezes boat design. That's a great way to ensure even racing but also a sure way to block technological progress. The One Design concept basically prohibits design innovation so it has to be viewed as a mixed blessing in terms of moving sailing ahead.

Sail's shift from commercial utility to racing frivolity has led to some awkward and unimaginative transitions. . When sail power's prime purpose was to carry cargo, cargo was used as ballast to solve the stability problem. That was very sensible, using what you had to carry for profit as the balance force to keep the ship upright. When the commercial focus was removed, sailing ships simply replaced operative cargo with inoperative lead. That worked, but what an uninspired solution. Weight is the first enemy of speed, which makes it illogical to begin any serious quest for improved speed with the automatic assumption of fixed lead for ballast. Limiting design vision to that tunnel is an unnecessary restraint that has confined sailing speed and popularity.

But enough of this historical debris, let's get on with some new thoughts and analysis.

The persistent problem that has forever challenged sailors is how to operate successfully in two interactive, often turbulent fluid mediums. The upper fluid, the air, is the **drive force**. The lower fluid, the water, is some six hundred times denser and serves as a **flotation force** and a **drag force.** The water holds you up by flotation, but holds you back by drag. The interface between these two fluids, the surface, is particularly complex because it is constantly agitated by **surface waves**, waves caused by both the wind and by the boat's own forward motion. Surface waves are a prime contributor to the speed inhibitions facing a sailboat.

How to extract forward progress from this interactive confusion is complex, because often the full force of wind and wave is directly opposed to the direction you want to go. In this case, the source of propulsion is perversely inclined to beat you back. The harder the wind blows the greater this counter force and the more agitated the supporting surface becomes. In many ways it is simpler to design an airplane or a submarine because each of those has an independent, controllable drive source, the engine, and each operates in just one fluid medium, air or water. Operating in just one medium gives you consistent characteristics. Operating in the zone where two fluid mediums interface, the surface, gives a sometimes baffling mix.

One of the first hydrodynamic rules that complicated boat design is the concept of "hull speed." Hull speed, which is numerically expressed by the formula 1.34 x the square root of the waterline describes the immutable limitation that governs the upper speed of displacement (non planing) hulls. By this rule, longer displacement hulls are always potentially faster than shorter displacement hulls. The reasons why behind this mandate are complex, but have mainly to do with the bow and stern waves that are automatically generated by any hull moving through the water. In a simplified explanation, longer hulls "stretch out" those speed stealing waves more than short hulls. No amount of extra engine power can alter these displacement hull speed limitations because the build up of bow and stern waves creates impenetrable water walls and the more power you add the more the hull just sinks into the hole between those walls created by bow waves and stern waves.

The key operative fact of this rule is that fair and slender hulls will reach "hull speed" more quickly and with less power applied than shorter or less fair hulls. Obviously there are strong, practical considerations that limit how narrow a hull can be and still retain some semblance of stability.

Planing hulls escape this hull speed formula limitation by rising up and riding over the bow wave, which quickly reduces the hull's wetted surface drag, a release resulting in higher speed and flatter wake. But obtaining this advantage requires lighter hull weight, significantly higher propulsion power and broad, flatter after hull shapes, which are much less efficient in rough seas or lower speeds. So those conditions disqualify planing hulls from practical cargo carrying use.

Multihulls can also escape the "hull speed" formulaic limitation by gaining stability through the conjoined use of two or three slender hulls whose slenderness would be prohibitively unstable in single hull configuration. But this multihull speed advantage requires wide beam, light weight and connecting bridge height sufficient to be free of wave slamming. Nonetheless, by their narrowness multihulls can avoid the "hull speed" trap and this allows them to be inherently faster then displacement hulls of similar length.

Another one of the obtuse laws of hydrodynamics decrees that a streamlined shape can go faster under water than on the surface. Nuclear submarines prove this—they are able to do seventy plus knots underwater, but on the surface that same horsepower nets them much less. For a more everyday example, watch the competitive swimmers who have only recently discovered they can go faster underwater, propelled by just a dolphin kick, than they can on the surface using both arms and legs. So in reality a swimmer could win the fifty yard dash entirely underwater. The only limiting factor to this better underwater speed is the danger of the oxygen debt the swimmer builds up. So to control this, swimmers are limited to the amount of pool length in which they can employ this underwater speed advantage. Way back when I was a competitive swimmer we didn't know this, so we would flail away on the surface when our starts and push offs would have been much better served by underwater dolphin kicks. Why didn't we figure that out? All you had to do was look at fishes and imitate their motion.

Actually sailboat design was long distracted by the shape of fast fishes. The reasoning, which seemed quite logical, was that the underwater shape of sailboats that wanted to go through the water fast should imitate the body shape of those fishes that observably swam fastest, the tuna, the barracuda, the mackerel, the dolphin. But that seemingly sound line of reasoning failed to take into consideration the different characteristics of surface waves. After all, fishes don't swim on the surface, so they don't have to contend with surface waves. This basic misunderstanding led to the adoption of the familiar tear drop shape waterline that replicated the shape of fast fishes. (Waterline shape is a horizontal slice of the hull taken at the waterline.) What throws the tear drop waterline shape all awry is the turbulent effect of surface waves, waves caused by wind and the boat's own motion.

The first effect of surface waves is pitching, the bobbing up and down that oncoming waves create. Pitching directly reduces forward speed and extreme pitching will stop a boat cold. It is easily observable that pitching is induced by the bow, which first meets the oncoming wave and is dampened by the stern. So fullness in the bow means the bow is pushed up more by flotation with each wave it meets. And narrowness aft or taper at the stern, means there is less flotation there to keep the stern from plunging down as the bow bobs up. The result is pronounced pitching, ergo slowness. Yet a full bow and narrow stern define the presumably efficient tear drop shape.

As it turns out, the best waterline shape for sailing is almost the exact reverse of the vaunted tear drop shape because it features a narrow bow entry forward and full stern sections aft. So the narrow sections forward tend to cut *through* the oncoming waves rather than be pushed *up* by them. And the full sections aft dampen and resist any downwind plunge by the stern. The result is less bobbing and smoother, faster speed forward.

Now just to confuse things when we are talking about underwater shape, shapes immersed in the water or airflow shapes in the air, the tear drop shape is correct. (Think wing tanks and bulb keels.) This is because they operate in just one fluid medium, free of the turbulent effect of surface waves. So in the case of underwater shapes there is much to be learned from the shape of fast fishes. We have come to realize that the most efficient, underwater shapes for rudders and keels closely match the crescent profiles found in the tail fins of tuna fish, whales and dolphins. It stands to reason that those fishes with the fastest tail fins would survive better than those with slower shapes, and so today's fishes and dolphins represent thousands of years of evolutionary tank testing.

Thus, natural fins deserve contemplation and emulation. Both the sails in the air, and the keel and rudder in the water are classified as *foils* and by foils we mean surfaces, which by their shape are capable of generating *lift*. Lift is most commonly recognized as the force that lifts airplanes off the ground. Lift operates at right angles to the foil. The most lift is generated by *high aspect ratio foils*, like glider wings. Aspect ratio refers to the length of the foil versus the width. Long, narrow,

9

high aspect ratio foils do a better job at creating lift than short, broad lower aspect foils. (See drawing. Pg. 15) This is because a high aspect ratio foil encourages more horizontal flow over the foil, with less tip loss than a low aspect foil.

Sailboats utilize lift in ways that are different and harder to visualize than airplane wings. Airplanes get their forward drive from engines and they really only need lift as an upward right angle force to get them off the ground and keep them in the air. Sailboats sailing to windward, against the wind, have to control the sidewards force of the wind, which wants to tip them over and push them sideways, in order to extract a small forward force to move them ahead. In recent years, we have learned how important it is to maintain the *verticality* of the foils, sails in the air or keels in the water, in order to maximize lift when sailing to windward. Any successful dinghy racer knows that he or she must hike hard to hold the boat flat to windward. Flatter is faster, but many sailors do not figure out just why this is so.

First off, you need to understand that when we talk about a keel or centerboard generating lift, that has nothing to do with lifting the boat out of the water. What a keel or centerboard needs to do is to create a shove to windward opposing leeway. It turns out that any surface, even a flat surface passing through a fluid, will create lift if it is carried at an *angle of attack.* To prove this to yourself, just stick your hand out the window of a moving car, hold your hand edgewise, then at an up angle. Your angled hand will feel an upward force, that's *dynamic lift.* Paper gliders and flat centerboards utilize dynamic lift because they present a flat surface at an angle of attack. A Laser or a Windsurfer hull presents a flat bottom at an angle of attack to movement through the water and *dynamic lift* causes the boat to *plane* or skim over the water.

Dynamic Lift, a surface held at an angle of attack is different from *aerodynamic* or *hydrodynamic* lift, which results from the different behavior of moving fluid passing over a curved surface. Thus the familiar airfoil shape of airplane wings, which are curved on the top side and flat on the undersides. In a simplified explanation, the air passing over the curved, upper surface of the wing travels faster because it has to travel a longer distance. This higher velocity creates lower pressure on the upper wing surface, resulting in a lift force upward.

So how can an airplane fly upside down when this lift from its upper curved surface is reversed? The answer is just that difference between dynamic lift and aerodynamic lift. Flying upside down with an angle of attack and engine power will create enough dynamic lift to keep the airplane up. But it's not nearly as efficient as aerodynamic lift.

For a more boat-oriented example of how lift works on a sail, go to a Windsurfer regatta. You will find Windsurfer sails strewn about, all set up on masts with their arched curves supported by tensioned battens and wishbone booms. Ask permission to hold a Windsurfer sail horizontally up over your head at right angles to the wind with the arched curve upwards and you will feel the sail literally try to lift you up. Conversely, hold the sail at right angles to the wind with the arched curve downward and you will feel the sail literally trying to press you down. Then watch a skilled Windsurfer execute a water start by holding his sail in the water at right angles to his floating board. The wind hits his arched wing and creates enough lift to pull him or her right out of the water and onto a standing position on the board. There is no better way to learn how the wind works than to learn to windsurf, because your body becomes the transfer medium that translates wind power to the hull and forward speed.

You should also understand how the forces vary when the foils stray from the vertical. As the foil in the air, the sail, heels over and away from the vertical in a gust, the lift force develops a downward component that presses the boat over even more. At the same time the foils in the water, the board, keel or rudder, lose part of their lateral resistance efficiency as the boat heels and they stray from the vertical. So the boat that is heeled more, slips more to leeward and inevitably loses to the boat that is sailed flat. You can easily prove this to yourself on the windward leg on a gusty day in any One Design race. Put yourself directly behind any boat that doesn't work to keep their boat flat. Under normal circumstances this is the hopeless position because the boat ahead backwinds the boat behind. But if you look ahead and spot an oncoming blast of wind, get ready to hike hard, point up and briefly ease the main to keep your boat flat you will see that the lazy boat ahead heels sharply to the puff and immediately slips to leeward.

Do this a couple of times and you will be free and clear to pass to windward.

This example reveals the flaw in the weighted keel approach to stability. A ballasted keel does not begin to exert its righting moment until the boat heels. The more the boat heels, the more righting force the keel exerts, but also the less lateral resistance it provides, resulting in slippage to leeward. So the keel only works for stability at the price of subtracting its efficiency in lateral resistance. This is an unfortunate trade off and this inherent deficiency of the fixed keel has led to new developments in the canting keel approach now employed by high performance ocean racers.

Instead of asking the keel to do what it traditionally has done, which is to *combine* the functions of stability and lateral resistance, where we know it can only succeed in the former by partially failing in the latter, the canting keel approach *divides* those duties. They have one or two high aspect ratio, unballasted daggerboards, whose job is to produce lift and lateral resistance, which they can very efficiently do as long as they are vertical to the waterline. To keep these daggerboards vertical is the task of the separate canting keel, which controllably swings its ballasted bulb directly out to either side where it provides an enormous righting force, which keeps the hull completely flat and the foils (sails and daggerboards) completely vertical. Thus the canting keel enables more sail area to be carried, with the hull and foils in the most efficient stance, resulting in large keel boats that can now plane across the oceans at previously unheard of speeds. It is estimated that new canting keel, monohull designs will reach top speeds over thirty five knots, which brings them into the previously unchallenged speed realm of multihulls. In the Volvo Race, Ericsson 4, skippered by Torben Grael set a monohull record, sailing six hundred two nautical miles in a day for an average speed of over twenty five knots.

This is very exciting progress, but the cost and mechanical complexity of the canting keel approach still place it outside the realm of practical application for wide consumer use. And it is important to note that multihulls still remain the ocean crossing speed champs. A large one hundred twenty foot catamaran recently set a twenty four hour record of seven hundred twenty miles. That's an average of thirty knots, which had to involve bursts over forty knots. The same catamaran set a new transatlantic record of four days, seventeen hours, with an average speed of twenty seven plus knots, all with no fuel consumption and no pollution. And a maxi catamaran holds the outright, non-stop, round the world sail record with a time of fifty days, sixteen hours, with an average speed of seventeen plus knots. There is no carbon fueled powerboat that can match that non stop performance.

Of course the technical racing rules are still in denial when it comes to some of these developments, for the rules still prohibit movable ballast. This rule is a bit laughable when you consider that the average maxi yacht has a twenty two person crew who religiously move from side to side with each tack. It they are not movable ballast, then why are they moving from side to side? Makes no sense, but then common sense has never played a leading role in the formation of racing rules, with resulting penalties to progress.

In any case, those designs that are unfettered by rules considerations have repeatedly shown that previously accepted performance limits can be consistently broken by innovative departures from the rules, which proves that open design is the key to new progress.

It is curious that many of the major breakthroughs in sailing design and popularity have come from outside the ranks of trained naval architects, and outside the channels of restrictive rules. For example, the Sunfish is numerically the all time most popular sit-down boat. It was put together in plywood by a couple of guys with a very simple idea, a board boat with the long established Lateen rig. It is now over fifty years old and still a great little boat whose longevity is solidly based on simplicity and the efficiency of flat bottom surfaces to create planing through dynamic lift. The eleven foot Moth is another small boat that has retained its vitality and spurred innovation by open rules that just limit the length of the boat and the sail area. Through intense owner inventiveness and hands on, skilled, amateur experimentation, the Moth, which began as a fast planing boat has evolved to be an even faster hydrofoil boat. This amount s to a whole new sailing skill and thrill and it is magical to see these Moths skimming along, above the surface, doing fifteen knots in a ten knot breeze.

Perhaps the best example of the *skilled amateur* design contribution came from Surfer and Surfboard maker Hobie Alter. His pioneer Hobie 14 was not the result of technical drawings or numerical calculations, rather he simply put together some surfboards, hand shaped them into asymmetrical hulls, then tested and refined them until he got it right. In so doing, he, more than anyone else, took the Polynesian multihull concept and advanced it into modern fiberglass production boats that became the most popular catamarans in the world.

I view Kite-Sailing in the same light, as a new sailing skill and thrill that brings spice and variety to the sailing menu. The fact that Kite Sailors are now the world's fastest sailors, with official speeds over fifty knots, adds luster to this new channel of sail power. And in terms of potential, this may be the most promising area of all because it automatically taps into greater wind velocity by virtue of its greater reach into the higher altitudes where the wind is inevitably stronger, a higher octane fuel if you will.

We have recently witnessed a legal wrangle (since resolved) where the Kite Sailing record was disputed by those who claim the shallow water employed in the new record setting may deliver a slight advantage due to a shallow water cushion effect. I view this as childish quibbling with an exciting new speed breakthrough. Instead of trying to beat this new speed standard, they choose to devise a rule that makes it illegal. The operative maxim here is that today's rules are tomorrow's anachronisms. So sailing should collectively tell the rule makers to get out of the way.

In this regard, one of my design precepts is that *simplicity is the ultimate sophistication.* It is always tempting to seek progress through greater complexity, which hides in the guise of sophistication. It is harder, but much more valuable to seek simplicity. But the *sophisticates* get defensive, as evidenced by the above brouhaha that wanted to take the speed record from the Kite Sailors who earned it. Drives them crazy to see one guy on a small board, flying a kite controlled by high tech strings, go faster than the most elaborate one hundred foot sailing machines. But that is prime evidence that *simplicity is the ultimate sophistication.*

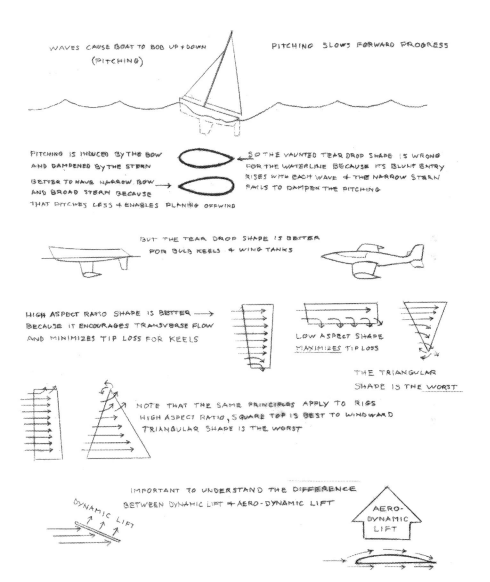

WAVES CAUSE BOAT TO BOB UP + DOWN
(PITCHING)

PITCHING SLOWS FORWARD PROGRESS

PITCHING IS INDUCED BY THE BOW
AND DAMPENED BY THE STERN

BETTER TO HAVE NARROW BOW
AND BROAD STERN BECAUSE

THAT PITCHES LESS + ENABLES PLANING OFFWIND

SO THE VAUNTED TEAR DROP SHAPE IS WRONG
FOR THE WATERLINE BECAUSE ITS BLUNT ENTRY
RISES WITH EACH WAVE + THE NARROW STERN
FAILS TO DAMPEN THE PITCHING

BUT THE TEAR DROP SHAPE IS BETTER
FOR BULB KEELS + WING TANKS

HIGH ASPECT RATIO SHAPE IS BETTER
BECAUSE IT ENCOURAGES TRANSVERSE FLOW
AND MINIMIZES TIP LOSS FOR KEELS

LOW ASPECT SHAPE
MAXIMIZES TIP LOSS

THE TRIANGULAR
SHAPE IS THE WORST

NOTE THAT THE SAME PRINCIPLES APPLY TO RIGS
HIGH ASPECT RATIO, SQUARE TOP IS BEST TO WINDWARD
TRIANGULAR SHAPE IS THE WORST

IMPORTANT TO UNDERSTAND THE DIFFERENCE
BETWEEN DYNAMIC LIFT + AERO-DYNAMIC LIFT

DYNAMIC LIFT

AERO-
DYNAMIC
LIFT

15

Chapter 2—Single Handed Sailing Skill

The ability to single hand a small sailboat cannot be disassociated from the ability to properly sail, it is **the essential basic skill**. To appreciate why this is true, consider the simple fact that the only way to begin the more complex task of piloting an airplane is by first learning to solo. And you can gain that more complex solo flying skill with an average of six to ten hours of instruction. I know this is true because I have done it. Further, I have talked with World War II veteran pilots who under the time urgency of war, were pushed into their solo test flight with as little as two hours of instruction. And remember, soloing an airplane is a potentially dangerous experience in which you can possibly kill yourself and wipeout several houses with a misstep.

By way of contrast, I know of no sailing school or instruction system that even pretends to start off with single handed instruction. Most sailing schools require at least a week of instruction with never any test or promise of delivering single handed skill. The customary practice is to place an instructor with three or four students in a small keel boat, and gradually build up steering and sail trimming skills. There are excellent economic reasons for this practice. First off, it is safe and non intimidating, nobody tips over and everybody stays dry and comfortable. Second, the expensive on board presence of the instructor is amortized over three or four students. And third, the deliberately extended time of instruction justifies the higher fees that are necessary to support the equipment, instruction and on water sites that the sailing school system requires. The alternative prospect of sending beginners quickly off by themselves poses unacceptable risks of capsize, collision, insurance and personal trauma, all of which conspire to make single handed instruction economically and emotionally non feasible. So we face the dilemma that delivering the best basic sailing skill is not possible under our present system of adult instruction. And in fairness, the standard system of sail instruction, as pioneered by a member of excellent schools and community sailing groups, has unquestionably done yeoman work in bringing the sailing experience to large numbers of people.

(Okay, Okay—three cheers for the status quo and the tried and true.) The problem is that the status quo system is not delivering the growth that sailing needs to become a better alternative to power. Sailing has been in numerical decline in the U.S.A. for at least the past ten years and doing more of the same is not going to change that. This doesn't mean that we have to abandon past practices, rather we need to preserve and invigorate them with some new approaches.

It will be a continual sub theme of this book that sail, the ancient medium of discovery, needs to rediscover and re-invent itself in new ways that better fit the modern world. Let's start with the recognition of some basic truths.

There is a vital synergy between the action of steering the rudder, the action of trimming the sail and the action of holding the boat flat, and only the single handed sailor fully gets this because only the single hander handles those tasks simultaneously and thus can feel first hand how action in one area directly affects results with the_other factors. When the duties of steering, trimming and hiking are separated, there is an inevitable decline in sensitivity to their essential synchronization. Of course in larger sail craft, those duties must be separated as a matter of practicality, but to breed the best sailors and to widen the network of sailing enthusiasm, single handed skill is a superior building block that cannot be ignored.

It follows that sailing needs a simpler sampling system, a way for the complete beginner to sip and savor the flavor of sailing in a totally safe and non intimidating fashion. It is an ironic paradox that virtually everyone agrees that the best way to start young kids sailing is in the Optimist pram. This is a small, stable *single handed* boat where children as young as seven can be safely taught to do everything one has to do to handle everything and go sailing by yourself. Perhaps best of all they learn self reliance and the confidence that being the solo skipper uniquely brings.

Yet when it comes to teaching adults, we abandon that advantage and force beginners into the team approach, which cannot deliver the vital, single handed skill that is the best way to set the hook for further sailing interest. It is no accident that the sports whose numerical popularity sailing most envies; golf, tennis, skiing, swimming and surfing, are all single handed sports. The lesson here is that sailing can be much more than just single handing, but just as you can't be a pilot until you can solo the plane, you can't really be a sailor until you can solo the boat. Single handing is the best skill, the best thrill and the best way to set the hook for future interest.

It is instructive to observe the rapid, recent growth of kayaking, which capitalizes on the lure of single handed control and links it with exercise, economy, car top convenience and natural quiet. Interestingly, almost fifty percent of the kayak market is female, a much higher percentage than sailing has ever commanded. There is an important clue there which the sailing world needs to recognize and exploit.

EXPO SOLAR SAILER

LOA	13'6"
BEAM	6'
DRAFT	2'6"
DISPL.	350 lbs.
S.A.	110 s.f

Chapter 3—Wanted—A Small Boat That Adults Can Quickly And Safely Single Hand

Together with help from Everett Pearson and Ted Hood, I attempted to answer this challenge with a small 13' dinghy, The Expo Solar Sailer. This boat had the following distinctive features: (See illustration)

1. The free standing, patented, self vanging Hoyt Boom, which allowed a single sail to be quickly furled, unfurled and reefed around a rotating mast.

2. A simple wind vane set over a disk divided into color segments. By checking what color segment the wind vane points to and matching the same color at the jam cleat for the color coded main sheet, correct sail trim angle was achieved.

3. A small electric motor with 3 speeds and reverse was built into the rudder aperture, with the throttle adjustment close to the tiller and a solar cell panel on deck to provide power.

4. A walkie-talkie radio, whereby an instructor on shore could talk to the beginner sailor and help guide them through initial difficulties.

The system was to first have the beginner sailor, at the dock, learn how to furl and unfurl and reef the sail. That would take about five minutes. The test group was three boats and twenty Navy wives who by their own admission, did not know how to sail. Next we'd ask them to turn on the small electric motor and depart the dock for some practice turns. Steering with a tiller takes some practice and learning with a quiet electric motor is much less intimidating than trying to learn to sail and steer at the same time. Once they've got the steering down, we would instruct them by radio to turn the Solar Sailer into the wind under electric power, using the deck mounted wind vane as guide. Students would then be told to unfurl the sail, sit on one side or the other, and bear off on the appropriate tack with the appropriate sail trim confirmed by the wind vane color disk. For all of this to work, the wind had to be under fifteen knots in order to avoid excessive heeling. Excessive heeling doesn't teach people, it just frightens them. You can't have fun while you're having anxiety, and having fun is the first priority that should trump other considerations in attempting to attract new participants.

Anyway, the experiment continued by carefully talking the students around an adjacent triangular course. Having more than one student out there trying seemed to help foster a feeling of camaraderie, sort of a comfort zone of shared trial. After each turn around the triangle, the student was guided by radio back to the dock. It is important to note here that the difficult mechanics of landing were avoided by simply telling the student to turn on the electric motor, turn into the wind, furl the sail and <u>drive</u> to the dock. We found that this was a necessary *safety valve* procedure that reassured the beginner that they could always get back with safety and *without embarrassment*.

After three coached by radio runs from the dock around the course and return to dock, the student was launched into the *unaided* solo run where they were told to just repeat what they had previously done. The radio contact support recourse was always available and some of the more timid beginners needed four to five guided tours before the solo. But the net was that all twenty of the beginners were able to handle the solo sail *on the first day* and they all enjoyed it. This prompt gratification was an important reward that enabled each student to honestly say and feel, "Yes, I sailed the boat all by myself on the first day." There was no attempt to portray this as a *complete instruction*, the important point was to quickly de-mystify the process and to quickly establish the skill and thrill of solo control. This is in marked contrast to the normal sailing school procedure, which is very gradual and *never* attempts to deliver the thrill and skill of the solo sail. Unfortunately, I was trying to *shorten* the instruction period, while most of the established sailing schools had a vested economic interest in *extending* it. So the project faced built in resistance from the sailing establishment and subsequently failed.

And I am not claiming that the *Solar Sailer* design was a totally satisfactory solution. The boat was too expensive and too tippy in heavy wind conditions. Fortuitously, there is now some new less expensive equipment available that can utilize the *Solar Sailer* lessons to better effect and I will get to that directly. One of the important by products of the Solar Sailer experiment was my realization of how pleasant and unobtrusive solar electric power is. There is no noise, no fumes, no starting hassles, just switch on the silent propulsion that in no way interrupts the important aesthetic rewards of sailing. So, instead of suffering through light wind slowness, you gain an entirely compatible, quiet speed boost, a feature that eases a lot of problems.

I should report that my experience in sailing instruction goes back sixty years to a very pleasant summer spent as sailing instructor at the Royal Bermuda Yacht Club in Hamilton, Bermuda. This historic yacht club is located in rather idyllic conditions on Hamilton Harbor with clear, warm water and good winds. The students were Bermudian kids from ten to fifteen, who were very attentive and far better mannered than most American kids. The boats were small plywood Firefly sloops, which were good performers, but a bit lively for beginners. The saving grace here was the incontrovertible fact that kids learn much more quickly, and with far greater adaptability than adults. So the teaching tactics for adults have to adjust to the slower learning patterns of adults, their lesser agility and their greater sensitivity to considerations of pride and embarrassment, all complicating factors. For example, tipping over is no big deal to a kid, they quickly learn to right the boat and scramble back aboard. Not so for adults, for whom a capsize is a traumatic, interest ending event.

What we face is a situation, a dichotomy, whereby the teaching practices in place for young children are working a lot better than our teaching systems for adults. In my hometown, Newport, RI, there is an organization, Sail Newport, that does a great job in general to promote sailing. I would say they are particularly successful with their youth programs with Optimist Dinghies. For example, it is not unusual to see a fleet of fifty or more Optis, all manned by boys and girls from nine to fourteen year olds, many with just first year experience, set forth to race on Narragansett Bay in brisk winds from fifteen to twenty knots. They depart the docks, sail out to the starting line, manage the start and several races and return safely to the dock. Of course there is ample, adult supervision and attending boats, but basically all these little people are out there on their own managing their own little boats in crowded circumstances and most importantly, having a good time. I cannot conceive of a similar situation with adults of one or two year's experience single handing a Laser or a Sunfish with equal equanimity. The penalty that this discrepancy reveals is that our present system of adult sailing instruction—for all their good intentions, do not generate the same level of skill or thrill that ten year olds can gain in their Optis.

So, without discarding or disparaging present efforts in adult sailing instruction, we need some new tool to introduce sailing to the wider audience of adult beginners. There is no better tool for expanding sail than parental interest and support, which means we need to expand the base of adult parent sailors who can then relay their enthusiasm and knowledge to their kids.

I believe the best boat currently available for quickly and safely delivering the thrill and skill of single handing to adult beginners is the Hobie Mirage Tri. It comes with the following unique advantages:

1. Reasonable price   4. Single sail simplicity

2. High durability   5. Unique pedal power backup

3. Stability of multi hulls   6. Reputable company support

By way of complete disclosure, the above is a completely non solicited endorsement, I have no financial connection with the Hobie Company. But I do own two of these pedal power kayaks and can testify to the reliability and efficiency of their very ingenious mirage drive. Coupled with a furling sail, the *mirage drive* makes leaving and landing a cinch. And no more worries about being hung up *in irons* or being caught drifting down on some fancy yacht. Pedal power is a totally reliable back up engine that always starts and never stalls. And multi hull stability removes the fear of capsize, which can be a total turnoff for the adult beginner.

What this means is that anyone can step aboard this stable trimaran, be comfortably seated and get immediately underway or out to clear water by simply pedaling, a skill everyone has. Then the sail is quickly and easily unfurled and voila, the beginner is sailing all by themselves with no fear of tipping over. So the beginner gets the instant reward of individual control and individual accomplishment. Quickly achieving this primal thrill of moving quietly with the wind is by far the best way to instill the desire to learn further. Correctly and ingeniously utilized, this can be a new catalyst to expand sailing.

Obviously there is a whole lot more to learn about sailing, but Americans like instant gratification. So why postpone the primal pleasure of the best thrill and the best skill, which is steering your own boat—all by yourself? Let's give them that first taste in the first outing and in so doing, bait them to learn more about the wider world of sailing with further instruction.

Chapter 4—The Sail Resort

Still missing from the equation, and it's a real missing link, is some new means of inducing adult beginners to try sailing in a way that will instill permanent interest. It's not as simple as just finding a boat, even one as well qualified as the previously described Hobie Mirage. It has to be a boat in a setting, attractive enough to transmit the all important atmosphere that sailing delivers to its advocates. To appreciate the importance of this, one has only to be old enough to remember the time, not too long ago, when skiing in the U.S. was a minor activity pursued almost exclusively by people in the North, who lived in or close to mountains. The sport was perceived as both difficult and dangerous and required enduring the discomfort of cold, plus the considerable exertion of climbing the mountain after each run, no ski lifts back then. Women had the good sense to largely absent themselves from this arduous scene, and the requisite hardiness of its few practitioners was matched by the awkwardness of their gear; bulky clothes, cranky skis, cumbersome boots and primitive bindings. Cold feet and broken ankles were common denominators of the sport. There were no international heroes or role models and no way for the general public to quickly sample the sport.

What changed all that was the rapid, sequential development of ski resorts with ski lifts, better equipment for rent and artificial snow to fill in when the weather didn't cooperate. Suddenly it was possible for anybody in any major northeastern city to drive on a weekend to a beautiful nearby resort, rent new, comfortable ski equipment, and get user friendly instruction that had them snow plowing down a gentle bunny slope in the first hour. Also offered was an active evening social life, where the shared sports experience established easy conversation and camaraderie. So at the bar the complete beginner could honestly boast, "Hey, I skied today, all by myself and it was easy." Women discovered they could look great in colorful, form fitting ski outfits and that women could ski just as well and often better than men. And kids with their lower center of gravity, became almost instantly proficient. To show the way forward, there were more challenging slopes, where more expert skiers could demonstrate the higher skill levels.

And so trying the sport of skiing was simplified into a weekend sampling in beautiful natural surroundings where an active evening social life assured anybody a good time and a non intimidating introduction to skiing was both the inducement and the reward. In short, the sport of skiing was attractively packaged as a getaway weekend of fun, in which the total beginner could be an instant participant and romance was an implied, if not guaranteed extra benefit. This combination would prove irresistible to a lot of attractive young people bored by the winter inactivity of city life. So a host of pretty women could rent weekend cars and take off to the slopes, dutifully followed by a host of young men whose visions of conquests were not limited to the slopes. So skiing became a new catalyst for romance and the hope of romance became a new catalyst for skiing, with the ski resort as the medium that made it all possible. The combustible mix of an exciting sport, natural beauty and romance was a sure fire source for word of mouth promotion and very suddenly skiing was *in* as an easily sampled and easily learned activity. And as beginners gained skill, there were other ski resorts to visit, and new equipment to purchase, and a whole new winter life style to explore. The key ingredient was driving proximity to major city populations.

And when snow boarding appeared, another natural, new market was created from every kid that had a skateboard or been a surfer. Of course skiing, strongly reminiscent of sailing, at first strongly resisted and even banned snow boarding, but they soon got wise and now snowboards represent over thirty percent of the slope action at ski resorts.

None of the above scenario is possible in today's world of sailing. If you want to take a course in sailing it is usually a week long, or several sessions process. Who wants to take a week long course in something they're not sure they'll like? And if you take the course, you will not get the vital reward of quick, solo accomplishment, or the built in supplementary social life. Nor will the equipment you are normally instructed in (keel boats over twenty five feet) be suitable as your initial first purchase entry to the sport. These are all hindrances, when what the sport needs are stimulants and easy economical first steps.

Given the strong outdoor similarities between the enjoyment of skiing and the enjoyment of sailing, it seems sadly short sighted for sailing not to have adopted the sail/ski resort formula concept that has been and is, so critical to the growth and sustainment of skiing.

Considering the complimentary, seasonal nature of both sports, skiing in the winter, sailing in the summer, there would seem to be a natural opportunity for established ski resorts, particularly those blessed with nearby lakes, to make economical use of their existing ski lodge rooms and restaurant facilities for summer *sail lodges*.

Basic equipment would be:

1. A fleet of ten Hobie Mirages to provide the quick, safe and easy reward of the solo sail.

2. A fleet of twenty Kayaks to introduce that sport and provide exercise for days with no wind.

3. A large, shallow sailing pool with large fans to make wind and to create an arena for model sailboats to race, maneuver and test sail when the weather doesn't cooperate.

4. A fleet of ten Windsurfers to teach that skill.

5. A fleet of keel sloops with spinnaker to teach that skill.

With those boats, competent instructors and starting with the solo sailing skill, it should be possible over the course of a weekend to introduce beginners safely and easily to basic sailing skills. Most important, the evening socializing would enable participants to interact and discuss the day's events. Guest speakers, celebrity sailors and exciting videos from ocean racing can further enliven the scene.

Properly and imaginatively developed, sail resorts could begin to play the same seminal role as ski resorts have and to provide the presently missing opportunity for large numbers of non sailors to quickly sample the sport. Obviously, the many existing charter companies, sailing schools, yacht clubs and community sailing organizations would be direct beneficiaries of this expanded group of people who have been favorably exposed to the skill and thrill of sailing by sail resorts.

Chapter 5—The New Nature of "Day Sailing"

The best sailors have traditionally come from the ranks of racing and/ or cruising, and understandably those categories received most of the attention from designers and the yachting press. Day sailing was sort of a marginal non category because it lacked competition or a specific purpose. But in recent years, experienced sailors found themselves increasingly frustrated by the way the time constraints of modern life did not mesh well with the increasing complications of both racing and cruising. They still had a strong interest in sailing, but meeting the demands of a fixed racing schedule and/or the hassles of lining up crew began to outweigh the pleasures. Some simply shrugged and went over to the dark side, but most sought a better way.

To meet this opportunity, a new boat emerged early in the 90's. The Alerion Express 28 blended the classic topside look from Herreshoff with a modern rig and underbody by Carl Schumacher, resulting in a new combination of sailing performance with single handed ease. This immediately struck a responsive chord with the cognescenti who rediscovered the simple pleasure of just going sailing by themselves or with friends on impulse. Equally important was the aesthetic reward, because this Alerion was quickly acknowledged as *the prettiest girl at the dance*®, a graceful yacht sailors instinctively paused to admire.

Now some ten years and four hundred plus boats later, the AE 28 has sparked its own line of good looking sisters with the AE 20, AE33 and AE38, plus a host of late coming, imitative competitors anxious to jump on the bandwagon. And Europe has now joined the parade with a number of new Day Sailer designs.

It is worth exploring some new realities that have fueled this trend.

1. Racing pleasure has to some degree been compromised by the logistics of large crews, the necessary presence of professional skills, the vacillations of the ratings rules and the ever escalating expense.

2. Cross this with the demands of family life and modern business and the result is a compression of time that requires a commitment many sailors are not willing or able to make.

3. Sailing offshore is a thrill best tasted as a memory. Once you've been there and done that, there's no need to reprove your manhood with rigors that, to mature view, are best left to the young. The unquestioned pleasures of relaxed cruising no longer demand the hardship of long destination voyages, when it is far simpler to charter the yachts of your choice in the most desirable locations in the Caribbean, Med or Pacific. This means owning a large cruising yacht no longer makes much sense for most sailors.

4. Most ladies prefer to dine and sleep ashore, and who can blame them? It is clearly observable that both the eating and the beds are significantly better ashore. Not to mention the availability of long, hot showers, laundry and wardrobe. So when you think about it, what sense does it make to try to recreate a floating home on the water when chances are you already have a much more comfortable home right on or near the water?

The net of these new realities is not that you should give up sailing, but rather that you might simply shift your sailing style to an elegant day sailer that simplifies and better serves your pleasures. The latest Alerions have carbon fiber spars whose strength allows the elimination of the backstay, enabling aerodynamically superior, full roached mainsails. This, coupled with the self vanging Hoyt Jib Boom creates new sail power that is fully efficient on all points of sail, easily handled by one person from the helm. This ushers in a new dimension of ease and swiftness to day sailing.

Together with my wife Donna, I directed the marketing and created all the advertising for the Alerion Express line for the years 1994 to 2007, and contributed significantly to the design effort during that period. Thus, I claim some credit for pioneering this new category of elegant Day Sailers, which I predict will continue to grow.

Chapter 6—Bring Back the Reach

In one of sailing's more doleful lapses, the reaching legs have basically been excised form the race course. The stated reason for this was that reaches were *just a boring parade with little chance of significant position changes.* I suspect that a more potent reason was the way the basic windward/leeward course simplified the work of the race committee. But to larger sight and for the pleasure of the participating sailors, which is the purpose of the exercise, what sense does it make to eliminate the fastest point of sailing from what is intended to be a test of sailing speed?

Let's grant the obvious, which is that for most keel boats, reaching legs do not offer the same potential for position change as a directly upwind or downwind legs. Unfortunately that lesser potential for gain or loss often led most sailors to the attractive option of relaxing in a straight line course with minimum sail trim change. And so, in a self fulfilling promise, everybody sailed the straight line course reaching course with minimum sail trim change, and very predictably, few boats changed positions. So the reasoning went, if there isn't going to be any position change, what is the point? Better to have more beating and running where position change is more dramatic.

What throws that seemingly logical reasoning out is the observable fact that the combination of skilled steering and appropriate accompanying sail trim can yield significant place change on the reach. I recall one vivid example where I saw George Bruder, the masterful Brazilian World Champion Finn Sailor, pass twenty two boats on the two reaching legs. The wind was too light for true planing, so Bruder concentrated on a zigzag course calculated to milk every passing wavelet for a small speed boost. Rather than placidly sitting still and steering straight, which was what everybody else was doing, he was a study in constant, synchronized motion geared to the waves. This meant he would constantly assess the slightly changing angle of the wavelets, and slightly bear off or head up to get the best *boost* angle from even the smallest wave. (I know all this because I was right behind him, deliberately copying his moves.) And of course each slight change in course angle required a slight change in sail trim, as well as a slight shift in body weight. The effect was a kind of jerky, but rhythmic choreography that resulted in erratic, but steady progress through the bewildered fleet. In today's world, an experienced judge might call this pumping, but it wasn't really, rather it was just quick coordinated adjustment in course angle and sail trim.

The net was that Bruder, the *master* went from twenty second place to first place with this highly specialized skill. And I, with lesser skill, gained twelve places and got back in the race. The point here is that this *reaching skill* is totally undeveloped by the current obsession with windward/leeward courses, resulting in lopsided sailing with a blind spot to the subtleties of reaching speed. I have often lamented that *Life Should Be A Reach*, but since that ideal is not possible we can at least protectively legislate the reach back into the picture.

So rather than dogmatically eliminating the fastest point of sail from the race course, let's ease sheets, watch the waves, steer smart and bring reaching back to its rightful place in the full spectrum of sailing skill.

Chapter 7—A Better Way for Olympic Sailing

For sailing to preserve its place in the Olympics, the governing solons of sailing must accommodate new realities and discard the burden of persistent delusions. This is important to the stature of the sport, which directly benefits from Olympic exposure and association.

For example:

1. Reliable wind over ten knots is the single most important element in conveying the grace of excitement of sailing. Light, fickle breezes introduce undesirable factors of luck and doom any coverage to acute visual boredom. So, future Olympic competition should insist on areas that provide good winds.

2. The essence of Olympic competition is individual achievement. That is confirmed by the leading popularity of events in track, swimming, gymnastics, skiing and skating, where the public can follow the action and identify with the individual athletes. Sailing should follow those successful examples.

3. It follows that it is neither necessary nor desirable for Olympic Class selection to attempt to represent all the varied aspects of sailing skill.

4. Like it or not, action that is friendly to TV will be increasingly important to permanent status as an Olympic event. The tactical

elements of sailing that are so fascinating and challenging to the participants are largely invisible or incomprehensible to the TV audience. So, while tactical sailing skill and the many classes that primarily reward that skill will deservedly remain the best choices for sailors in general, those are not the best choices for any hopes of Olympic survival. Recognizing this is not pandering to TV, but rather simply adjusting to the new realities of Olympic coverage.

For example, to insist on the inclusion of female match racing in Ynglings amounts to a foolish fixation on an arcane and visually unexciting aspect of the sport. Likewise, the venerable Star Class is inappropriate because the cost and complexity of the equipment, like the weight of its crew, is too heavy. And given the Olympic goal of *higher, faster, stronger*, why should we exclude multihulls, which are demonstrably one of sailing's fastest forms? With all these thoughts in mind, here are my recommendations for future Olympic Classes:

- **The Foiling Moth**: Surely these are the most exciting new boats on the sailing scene, requiring an entirely new mix of strength, balance and steering skill and delivering an entirely new look to sailing.

- **The A Cat**: Simple, but very sophisticated, these lively trapeze single hand Catamarans are faster than any of the current Olympic classes.

- **The Windsurfer**: How can they not be included? But make their minimum starting breeze be 12 knots to reduce the pumping factor.

- **Kite Sailing**: This is now the fastest sailing of the future, as physically exacting as it is visually spectacular. But forget the traditional Olympic Course, give them a straight Ocean Triangle that begins and ends on the beach, going out and in through waves.

- **A new 15', all carbon, sit down, single sail, planing dinghy:** To replace the Finn and the Laser—admirable classes that have earned their retirement in favor of new technology.

These recommendations would reduce Olympic Sailing line up (and expenses) to a more manageable 5 classes, each with male and female divisions. Youth and athleticism would be highly favored, as they should be in the Olympics. All of the traditional forms of sailing would benefit from the emphasis on individual sailing skill, which automatically creates new avenues of simplicity that provide needed balance to sailing's confining image of complexity.

Given the ossified thinking that prevails in the upper ranks of sailing regulators, ideas like this are likely to be resisted. But the dogmatic replication of conventional sailing competition will predictably result in the elimination of sailing from the Olympics. New action has its risks, but inaction is the biggest risk of all.

For example, taking a cue from track and swimming, how about adding the visual interest of a medley relay race to the sailing competition? Each relay team to be comprised of a Foiling Moth, an A Cat, a Windsurfer and a sit down planing hull dinghy. Watching these singlehanders handle the maneuvering involved in passing a baton over a short course, would make for highly exciting, easy to follow sailing action, ideally suited to television.

Chapter 8—The Computer Assisted Atrophy of the Mind's Eye (CAAME)

Before we completely capitulate to the all seeing eye of the almighty computer, let me strike a defiant blow in favor of the free hand sketch powered solely by the magic of the mind's eye. I recognize that this failure to bow submissively to a clearly superior deity will brand me as a retrograde dinosaur doomed to incipient extinction. So be it. Let the record show that I went down swinging my obsolete pencil and my non digitalized imagination. And I continue to doubt the belief that computers can conjure certainty out of subjects that are laden with uncertainty. Perhaps the most insidious effect of CAAME is the computer assisted homogenizing of design thought. Most designers employ the same computer design programs, which do consistently produce excellent results. Unfortunately the byproduct of that consistency is a regimented uniformity of design appearance and performance. Using the same computer program consciously and unconsciously tends to lead everybody down the same paths, which discourages individuality and open experimentation. When it comes to encouraging fresh thinking, nothing beats a blank sheet of paper and a pencil guided by the mind's eye. I find it dismaying that many modern designers don't even know how to draw!

As I visit the modern design office and see droves of what appear to be bright young people bent slavishly over blank or blinking computer screens, I am seized with a desire to shake them vigorously and admonish "never mind what that damn screen says—what do you think?" Of course the best this might net me would be a condescending sigh and a semi patient explanation that the computer can correctly do in a flash, what it will take me weeks to calculate, with a high probability of error. Faced with this grimly accurate logic, I retreat to stubbornness. I counter by questioning the computer's ability to entertain the unlikely, or embellish the idle flight of fancy, or to visually contemplate a concept, or compose a passionate love letter. In short, I worry that we are cultivating a generation that may be losing, for lack of exercise, the mind's eye's unique ability to instantly create a vivid scene from a descriptive phrase or a wandering, reflective thought.

For example, I am discouraged when my efforts to induce my grandchildren to read *Robin Hood* are greeted with the explanation that *they already saw the movie.* Don't they understand that at age twelve my mind's eye had already created a very complete and vivid picture of Sherwood Forest and Little John and Maid Marian, a scenario far superior to the best efforts of Hollywood. And my mind's eye's personal, clear picture of Robin Hood beggars Kevin Costner's earnest portrayal. Best of all, I both enjoyed and benefited from the exercise of my imagination, man's best tool for invention.

So, when I see a young person out on a boat on a sunny day intently absorbed in the mindless intricacies of some computer game, oblivious to the surrounding spectacular nuances of wind and wave, I wonder at modern sciences' perverse ability to distract from the natural wonders. To my list of computer related frustrations, let me add another acronym, <u>CISC</u>, which stands for *Computer Induced Sense of Certainty.* How often do we see and feel comforted by the statement *computer designed,* which we are trained to take as the reassuring endorsement of some impeccable higher authority. Yet in my personal design experience, the worst design I ever participated in was one where I abandoned my own personal judgment in favor of elaborate and sophisticated computer projections, all generated by a very proficient computer expert, who in the final analysis was nothing more than a skillful charlatan. So, I signed off on the design, overpowered by reams of computer based certainties, all of which bespoke a scientific precision that seemed far above my elementary knowledge, but most of which turned out to be sham and illusion, cleverly clothed in computer certainty.

My second encounter with CISC came in the recent 2009 financial debacle, where I was lured to participate in a financial scheme, generated by two learned MIT Professors, who claimed to have a computer based formula able to gauge and profitably adjust to variations in the stock market. Again, masked by *sophisticated* hyperbole, which my own failure to comprehend somehow translated into exaggerated respect, I was bamboozled and financially scalded. These painful examples lead me to yet another acronym, CBARD, *Computer Based Abdications of Reasonable Doubt.*

The lesson here is that the unmatched and unquestioned value of the computer can be dangerously dependent on the judgment and motives of the operator and that computer based projections that provide you with the answer you want to hear are tempting but forbidden fruit.

But hush, these are clearly subversive thoughts, for which some computer controlled government agency could have me committed. Best I retreat to my private vault of personal recollections, an isolated but superior vantage point that armors me 'gainst the depredations of modern gadgetry. I take refuge in my antique respect for the superior writings of Shakespeare and the superior drawings of DaVinci, and in the hope that human ingenuity is still the best master of our fates.

Chapter 9—The High Cost of Low Price Petroleum

It is vital to discard at the outset, the popular delusion that low cost petroleum helps the economy, or conversely that high price fuel hurts the economy. The more operative reality is that in the U.S.A., price is the determining factor governing the volume of fuel consumed. So high fuel price means lower fuel use and lower fuel price means higher fuel use. And the by-product pollution penalties of higher use, clearly outweigh the short term benefit of lower price. In addition to the obvious increases in pollution that low cost/high use brings, there is the perverse secondary effect of sabotaging attempts to introduce and improve the necessary alternative fuels of wind and solar. Equally damaging, is the way that low price fuel lures the ever gullible American buyer back to the folly of big gas guzzling vehicles, aided and abetted by Detroit's complimentary myopia in car design.

All of this leads inexorably to the need for a U.S. fuel tax that will put enough of a floor under the carbon fuel price to allow the alternative solutions of wind and solar to succeed with gaining the energy independence that is clearly desirable. Virtually all the European countries employ fuel taxes for all the above reasons, and they manage to survive quite nicely. Unfortunately, Americans feel we have a God given right to the cheapest fuel in the world, and faced with that, none of our politicians have the courage to propose the fuel tax that the situation clearly calls for. Until that happens, we will continue to be at the mercy of the Petro Dictators in the Middle East and Venezeula, who will continue to manipulate the oil prices in ways that assure our continual addiction. This is a sad merry-go-round that we must get off. By nature of their recreational choice, sailors, rowers, canoeists and kayakers are more sensitive to this need than the general public and can thus be a useful catalyst to the necessary change. But we must take a stand and raise voice and votes to the cause. Do not underestimate the power of social scorn to reach even those billionaires to whom price is no object. Social scorn can make carbon fuel use unfashionable long before high prices makes it impractical and we need both deterrents to attack the global scourge of carbon fuel pollution. Do not be distracted by the small twenty cent per gallon taxes being proposed by some states to alleviate their budget shortfall. That's not enough and it's for the wrong reason.

Chapter 10—What Need For Speed?

The truth is, in recreational sailing there is no intrinsic need for speed. I say this somewhat shamefacedly, because back in the 90's I authored a series of articles titled *The Need For Speed*, which chronicled and extolled speed progress in sailboats. I remain personally firm in my preference for lively sailboats as opposed to sluggish sailboats. And I follow with great interest, the dramatic speed advances; kite sailing, foiling moths, multihulls and ocean crossing sprinters. And for those who really want significant speed under sail, hop aboard an iceboat and hold your hat. Or more accurately, tighten the chin strap on your helmet. For those seeking speed thrills, sail power can indeed offer a whole new realm of natural, non polluting excitement.

But to larger sight, one has to confess that the actual speeds that are reasonably attainable under sail on the water remain puny alongside power boats, and are probably destined to stay that way. Note I say actual speed as opposed to perceived speed because if you have ever planed a Laser at twelve knots, you think you are flying at about thirty knots. And windsurfers and multihulls that approach and exceed twenty knots generate a heightened perception of speed that far exceeds the actual speeds obtained. Kite sailors are in a speed world of their own, with bursts of exhilarating airborne independence.

The point here is that a preoccupation with power and speed is what led us down the less than garden path to petroleum addiction. And just as young people must learn, often the hard way, that actions have consequences, so the recreational boating world must learn to consider the heavy environmental consequences of high speed on the water, which to informed sight, far outweigh the highly temporary thrills of high speed on the water.

Coolly analyzed, high recreational speed under power on the water serves no useful purpose, and gives rise to a confluence of calamities, present and future. If we will but widen the spectrum of our sensory perceptions, sailing offers a very wide range of satisfactions at lower speed. And it is the developing of the refined set of skills necessary to coax a sailboat from four knots to four plus knots that are the intensely fulfilling reward. That may sound tame, but it isn't.

After all, any damn fool can push the throttle down and thereby create high speed that is totally unrelated to skill. That is the false God that we must stop worshipping. Those terminally attached to the convenience of throttle control must re-tool and learn to appreciate the nuances of the passing marine scene that requires close attention, which in turn requires slower speed for full appreciation. Solar Electric power will enable environmentally kind speeds with environmentally blessed rewards, and that is the only speed that recreational boating really needs.

As a side note, over the years I have observed that in general, the brainpower of the skipper is inversely proportionate to the horsepower of his engine. Passing time has repeatedly validated that assessment. It is not accidental that Sailing was Einstein's choice for recreational relaxation. And it is not unrelated that Darwin developed his seminal theories on natural selection as a result of his five year sailing time on the *Beagle*, an experience totally dependent on the free and inexhaustible nature of their wind fuel supply. And John Masefield's haunting poetry "I must go down to the seas again" derived directly from his years on a sailing vessel. Sailing experience similarly influenced Conrad, Melville, Drake, Nelson, Magellan and countless others who were obliged to work with nature without punishing it.

Parallel examples of intellectual revelation resulting from high speed powerboat voyages do not spring to mind. In short, the processes of solving sailing's operational challenges were inextricably interwoven with the historical processes of exploration and discovery and that heritage infused sailing with an inbred system of curiosity, inquiry and contemplation. It follows that recreational sailing need not be dependent on the pure pursuit of speed, because it is the pleasure of the pursuit, and not its velocity that remain the lure.

Chapter 11—The Cascading Connectivity of Things

Consider the sport of surfing. As a youth I spent my happy summers at the Jersey Shore, swimming and riding waves. Of course we thought of surfing primarily as body surfing in with the waves. From that we progressed marginally to surfing by lying on wooden planks, which were called surfboards. The addition of swim fins gave us more starting power and some ability to angle across the face of the wave, but basically you just tried to catch the wave before it crested and then you rode it straight down to the bottom of the wave, at which point you were engulfed by the breaking foam. But then with the help of swim fins you could spurt ahead of the wave again and ride it to shore. Great fun, but pretty basic.

Of course the Hawaiians were way ahead on this and stalwarts like Duke Kahanamoko, many years ago, would stand up on long mahogany boards and ride big Pacific swells for considerable distances to shore. But they were still basically riding the waves straight in. The advent of foam and fiberglass opened up the way to smaller, lighter boards and rear fins added new ability for steering and control. So now with skill, a surfer could pump hard, catch the swell before it broke, jump to his feet, take the drop and angle sharply across the face of the wave away from the break and in effect be constantly accelerating on a clean slope. This is a magical sensation and having surfed big waves in Puerto Rico and Hawaii, I can report that this is one of the most exciting, physical thrills one can experience. And to see Laird Hamilton now ride fifty foot monster waves away from the break, often in the "tunnel," with tons of water arching over him is awe inspiring.

From when I started surfing in the 1940's, the sport has progressed to the point that now, here in New England, surfers surf year round in wet suits, often finding keen excitement from standing up on very small waves that still generate that unique surfing thrill. So it has only taken seventy years for us to come somewhat close to what the Hawaiians figured out one hundred fifty years ago.

Okay, at this point think about the "connectivity" of what surfing skill has generated. When surfers became bored and restless on waveless days, they started fooling around to create surfing on land. They took short planks to which they fastened roller skate wheels, which allowed the rider on the plank to roll along down hill. The problem was that those all metal wheels were noisy and high friction and being fixed made them hard to turn. By this time, pioneers like the Harkens had shown how plastic ball bearings could radically reduce friction in pulleys and turning blocks that would spin freely with much less effort. So California surfers took that technology into new plastic wheels that would spin quickly, quietly and easily. And to aid turning, they gave these wheels flexible rather than fixed mountings.

This breakthrough led directly to the new sport of skate boarding, wherein agile youths could propel themselves on level roads with great speed and maneuverability, all enabled by wheels that would spin better. I recently picked up one of the modern skate boards with soft, quiet urethane wheels and with the flick of a finger the wheels would spin freely for sixty seconds. Then some imaginative ice skaters visualized that four of these free spinning wheels, placed in line on the sole of an ice skate boot, could on land, replicate the glide of a metal blade on ice. Bingo, the new sport of in line *blading* was born, and blossomed. Connectivity.

Meanwhile, out on the snow ski slopes it took some skiers more time than it should have to figure out what surfers, skate boarders and single ski water skiers already knew, that a single plank might do on snow what two skis had conventionally done—glide, turn, jump and maneuver with a new kind of speed and grace. Of course the skiing establishment strongly resisted this single ski heresy, which was initially banned on many ski slopes. But the young people flocked to this new way to "surf" the snow, utilizing body moves that stemmed directly from surfing. And so "snow boarding" evolved directly from surf boarding and quickly gained broad popularity that was eventually confirmed by status as a new Olympic sport.

Meanwhile, on the sailing front, as discussed elsewhere, multihulls sailboats were slowly gaining overdue recognition. Mind you, this was many years after Captain Cook's Pacific sailors on board their "modern" square riggers, noticed that the primitive natives could sail circles around them on speedy multihull craft that were really just hollowed out logs, spread apart and lashed together. Since they had no access to the saws necessary to create ribs and planking and single logs by themselves were too rolly, they simply intuitively made good with what they had and spread the logs apart for the stability necessary to effectively carry sail.

Thus the "primitive" Polynesians made the design breakthroughs leading to the multihulls that are today the world's fastest ocean going sail craft, as well as inventing the wave riding surfboards that subsequently spawned skate boards, in line skates, snowboards, windsurfers and kite sailors who could sail to record breaking speeds over fifty knots. Pretty good for some uneducated natives with no engineering degrees, no computers and no metallurgical skills. Proving yet again that simplicity is the ultimate sophistication and that the complexity often encouraged by advanced learning can also encourage and falsely legitimize lesser solutions.

Part II
Design Solutions

Introduction

In Part II, I will attempt to convert some of the ideas and principles discussed in Part I to actual designs. By this I am not suggesting that these are the only or even the best solutions, they are simply my ideas, which if nothing else may serve to entertain or to prompt other ideas. I have taken the liberty of accompanying my ideas with illustrative sketches, because in my view nothing beats a drawing to clarify a concept.

I believe it is fair to summarize the progress in sail in simplified terms, as proceeding from the Square Rig to the Gaff Rig to the Marconi Rig. It is oddly refreshing that some of the newest high performance rigs are now borrowing the square head from the oldest rigs. And I have discovered new virtues in a new version of the Gaff Rig that everybody had dismissed as antique. I have the least enthusiasm for the Marconi Rig—which I believe to be fatally flawed by its insistence on the inherently inefficient triangular plan form, which is "The worst possible shape the aerodynamist could invent." Even the brilliantly primitive efforts of the Wright Brothers grasped this basic aerodynamic fact, and they went with rectangular plan form wings. Good thing because they never would have gotten off the ground with the triangular plan form wings.

The fact that the sailing world has for many years embraced for its "wings" the inefficient triangular shape that the Wright Brothers rejected, speaks volumes for the shortage of practicality and imagination that has afflicted the field. Let's get into that.

Chapter 1—Back To The Future—The Square Rig Returns

As stated, I believe it is fair to summarize the progress in sailing rigs, in simplified terms, as proceeding from the Square Rig to the Gaff Rig to the Marconi Rig. But just when we had comfortably consigned Square Rigs and Gaff Rigs to antiquity, square headed rigs began showing up on the fastest windsurfers, multihulls, ocean racers and America's Cup challengers. And I have discovered some new efficiencies for the Gaff Rig. So what's going on? Well, nothing that a little more careful study of aerodynamics would not have rather quickly revealed. As authority, C.A. Marchaj pointed out in his comprehensive study, *The Aerodynamics of Sailing*, "The worst imaginable planform that the aerodynamist could possibly invent is the triangular one." But how can that be when the shape most commonly seen on sailboats is the triangle, "the worst possible planform?" For sailing's better future, wouldn't we be better off starting with the *best* possible shape, rather than the *worst*?

Let's analyze how we got to where we are. The currently popular Marconi Rig, which is demonstrably faster than the Gaff Rig that preceeded it, is based on a system of highly tensioned wires, creating a triangular trap between forestay and backstay, which confines the jib and the main into the aforesaid "worst possible shape." And by way of concomitant problems, this system of highly tensioned wires places heavy compression loads on the mast, which basically becomes a stressed ram being forcefully thrust into the bottom of the boat, while simultaneously trying to bend up the ends of the boat. To counteract these formidable forces requires a lot of additional strengthening in the hull, as well as a maze of spreaders, upper and lower stays, all charged with keeping the highly loaded mast "in column," an optimistic assignment given that the failure of any part of any one of these highly stressed elements will send the whole works tumbling down. Hardly a simple solution.

Back in 1976, when defending the free standing spar to introduce "Freedom Yachts," I pointed out, as an ex-pilot, that "They used to put wires on airplane wings, but they don't do that anymore." However, sailors had trouble accepting the simple logic of that, and habit dies hard in the sailing world.

And in fairness, there was established evidence to the windward superiority of the Marconi Rigged sloop, which was totally dependent on a system of tensioned stay wires. Here, it is important to note the basic truth that the presence of any mast severely penalizes the performance of the sail behind it. This is why sail area in the jib, which has no mast disturbance in front of it, is twice as effective as sail area in the mainsail. So since a free standing mast must have a larger diameter in order to have the strength to stand free, its penalty of mast interference was inevitably greater, resulting in lesser performance to windward. Balancing and compensating for that was the fact that the free standing mast's removal of the backstay allowed more sail area via a more efficient curved roach, which led to better performance reaching and running. So it was a trade off. But sooner or later, all cat rigs, including cat ketches and cat schooners have to admit the windward superiority of the sloop, which can be traced to the jib's clean leading edge and the narrower diameter of the stay supported mast.

This advantage is artificially inflated by the nature of the modern race course—which in most cases is strictly windward/leeward. Since the windward legs necessarily involve the delays of tacking and the longer distance of a zig zag course, inevitably more time is spent there and therefore boats that are faster to windward, ergo sloops, generally win most races.

So, naturally and somewhat unfortunately, design attention tends to disproportionately focus on those elements that lead to better windward speed. I say "unfortunately" because in the real world where day sailers and cruisers outnumber racers—very few would voluntarily choose to spend most of their sailing time beating to windward.

"Gentlemen do not cruise to windward" is the oft quoted phrase that confirms this. Yet many of the features and habits developed for racing tend to influence all sailboats and not always to their benefit. A prime example would be the IOR Rule, whose perverse influence infected the sailing scene for many years. Back then, I identified the IOR rule as " Inverted Offshore Reasoning", which it certainly represented, with pointy ended boats that were laden with bad habits and unsafe sailing characteristics. Fortunately, the IOR eventually fell victim to the burden of the bad design tendencies it encouraged— but it took a long time and was a costly detour. Rules have a way of blocking and confining the free thought that is vital to design progress, and much of sailboat design has been shackled to rules.

Another rule controlled racing fashion that has unduly affected sailing is what I call "the curse of the genoa jib." The genoa, as we all know is an overlapping jib, which gains helpful extra sail area, via the overlap, within the triangular trap. What many do not know is that the genoa jib owes its early popularity to the fact that the ruling powers decided that the overlap area, which was the key to the genoa's success, would not be penalized, not counted in the boat's rating. This "freebie" was quickly pounced on by designers, and by anybody who really wanted to win races. Because all things being equal, an overlapping genoa will always beat a non overlapping jib, particularly to windward in light air, simply because its larger area generates more power.

The problem, the curse of the genoa jib, stems from a series of intractable complications.

1. By its overlapping nature, the genoa cannot utilize the mechanical assist of blocks at the clew, because they would bash themselves to pieces with each tack. So massive, expensive winches, plus operator strength are required for the work of winching, an arduous process for which unfairly penalizes females who lack upper body strength.

2. The simple act of tacking a genoa involves gingerly releasing a highly tensioned sheet line on one side, and then quickly recapturing the sheet on the other side, a tricky, labor intensive, troublesome task that complicates sailing and denies the pleasure of single handing.

3. The genoa dramatically loses power as its sheet lines are eased, since the leech twists off uncontrollably. Dead downwind, the genoa becomes completely useless, just slatting about and making a noisy nuisance of itself. So offwind, where *more* sail power is required, the genoa delivers *less*.

4. The only solution to the genoa's downwind inefficiency involves the foredeck work of several experienced crew to either set a whisker pole or a spinnaker—the latter being one of the more hazardous procedures in sailing.

Thus, one design defect is propped up by the addition of others and as a final evasion of common sense, the exaggerated number of crew required to handling the genoa and spinnaker are justified as movable ballast, which the rules specifically prohibit! Alice In Wonderland and Rube Goldberg would feel right at home is this scenario.

There has to be a better way. So let's explore some other possibilities, guided and informed by two basic realities:

1. The square headed sail profile is inherently superior.

2. A clean leading edge has proven advantages.

So, just what is behind this superiority of the square headed rig? How real and how significant is the improvement versus the currently popular pointy headed rig?

The best pragmatic proof of the performance superiority of the square headed rig comes from the clearly observable fact that all the fastest sailboats now employ it. From Windsurfers to Kite Sailers, to Multihulls, to Ocean Racers and America's Cup challenges, the square headed rig is now de riguer, mandatory. This is not some stylistic fad, or rule induced favor, but a clear cut performance edge that is measurable in better boat speed achieved. The real wonder is why it took us so long to figure this out. Part of the answer lies in the relatively minor speed gain involved. Saying that the triangular rig is inferior, which it is, does not alter the reality that many sailors are very happily sailing triangular rigs and the fractional gains offered by the square rig are not sufficient to induce them to change.

But for your better understanding of sail power potential it is important to understand why the square rig is inherently superior to the triangular rig. In a simplified explanation, the triangle shape creates more induced drag and tip vortices that interfere with the transverse air flow necessary to generate lift. Which is why you never see triangular wing tips on airplanes. In contrast, the rectangular plan form with square tip *encourages transverse air flow* and *minimizes tip loss*, which is why you regularly see square wing tips on airplane wings. And because air and water are both fluids, this same characteristic behavior also explains why a deep, high aspect ratio keel is better to windward than a shallow, low aspect keel—or a triangular keel. It gets down to encouraging transverse flow and discouraging tip loss. The earlier drawings illustrate how this works, both for foils (sails) in the air and for foils (keels) in the water.

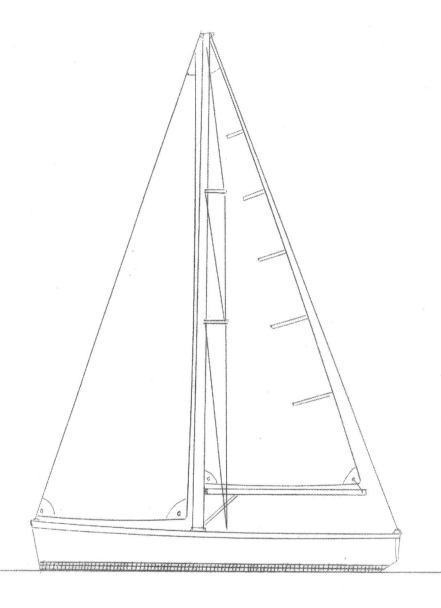

"The worst imaginable planform, which the aerodynamicist could possibly invent is the triangular one." —C.A. Marchaj

"Yet most sailboat designs persist in embracing the triangular rig."

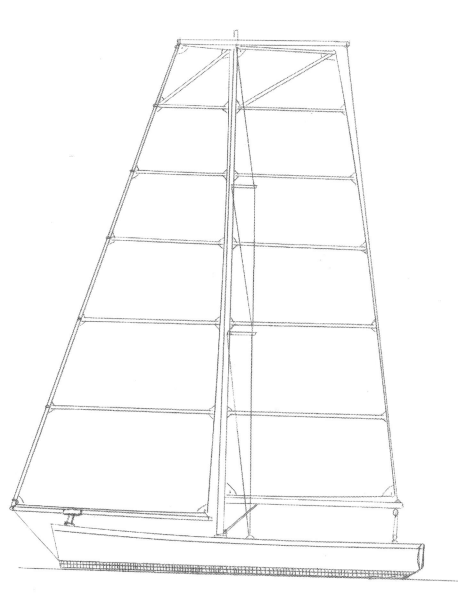

"So why settle for the worst possible shape when the
square head sail is demonstrably better?"

Chapter 2—The Hoyt Offset Rig (HOR)

The relative efficiency of the jib versus the main (twice the power for the same area) can be largely traced to the jib's advantage of a clean leading edge versus the mainsail's inherent penalty of mast induced interference. Taking note of these realities, I was tantalized by the possibility of combining the simplicity of a single sail with the aforesaid virtues of the square rig and the clean leading edge. With an earlier prototype labeled the Delta Rig, I had already experimented with the mast in the rear of the boat to achieve the clean leading edge. But the drag of the extensive rear rigging required, and the difficult of obtaining sufficient luff tension seemed to defeat any marked advantage, and the project languished.

So I ruminated. If the mast ahead of the sail inevitably penalizes the sail behind, and putting the mast behind creates a separate set of problems, what about putting the sail off to the side, creating an offset rig?

My many years sailing a Sunfish helped here because the Sunfish lateen gaff and boom are carried off to the side of the mast and the boat sails passably well on either tack. But one tack distorts the sail as it presses against the mast, making that tack slightly slower, which is annoying. So, I decided to design and patent a rotating strut that set the boom well away from the mast, far enough away so that even on the "bad" tack the sail is free and clear of mast interference.

At first glance this admittedly looked a little weird. But test sailing a 20 ft. prototype with the HOR (Hoyt Offset Rig) immediately demonstrated that the wind doesn't really care about the centerline, proof being that boat sailed equally well on both tacks. This really should not have been the surprise that it was. After all, when a catamaran sails at speed, with one hull lifted out of the water, the mast and sail are no longer on the centerline, they are offset in relation to the working hull in the water.

For an ever more dramatic example, consider the world's fastest sailboat, the kite sail, where the sail is carried 20 or more yards to leeward and completely separate from the hull. Once I got over the initial "unusualness" of the offset rig, a number of specific advantages emerged.

First, the balance factor, with approximately ¼ of the sail area ahead of the mast, markedly reduced the weather helm for which catboats are notorious. Second, the force of the jibe is reduced by the same balance factor, because the forward part of the sail acts as a brake to slow the swing of the boom. And third, having the boom off to one side cleared up the cockpit area because you don't have to contend with the boom in the middle, where it hits your head every time you stand up.

What about the permanent rotating gaff aloft? Well, that is necessary as a support system for the square headed sail. Don't worry about the weight and windage, all I've really done is to take the top triangular tip section of the mast and sail, (which is essentially useless aerodynamically) and convert it to a horizontal gaff. This offers less windage to windward and actually lowers the center of gravity and creates efficient extra sail area aloft where there's always more wind.

Also interesting is the way this horizontal gaff can be utilized as an efficient lever arm to tighten the forestay and thereby the luff. To achieve this there is a permanent forestay connecting the front of the boom and gaff, and a permanent backstay connecting the rear of the boom and the gaff. This feature insures that the boom and gaff will act in concert, without the wasteful "twist off" that penalizes the conventional gaff. And by simply trimming down on the mainsheet, the backstay on the rear of the boom pulls strongly <u>down</u> on the rear of the gaff, which acts as a lever arm through the fulcrum at the mast head to pull strongly up on the forward part of the gaff, thereby tensioning the forestay and gaining the luff tension that is necessary for good windward performance.

While it is true that the wind doesn't really care about the centerline (nor do keels or rudders), it is not true that both tacks with the Hoyt Offset Rig are exactly the same in terms of performance to windward. The change factor here is what I term the lateral center of effort in the rig. Most are familiar with the vertical CE, and moving the rig off to one side does not materially affect that. What is affected by change in the lateral CE is the heeling moment. Once of the first things I noted with the experimental HOR on a 20 footer was that the "bad tack", the tack that puts the sail close to and often pressing against the mast, produced markedly *less heeling.* Yet both tacks seemed equal in terms of speed. This initially didn't make sense because putting the mast where it could interfere—even slightly with the clean airflow over the vital leeward side of the sail—that tack would have to be slightly slower to windward. Even though my Offset Rig usefully mitigated that effect, it's still there. What compensates for this deficiency is the advantage of reduced heeling produced by carrying the sail to windward of the mast. And there is a way to harness that slight advantage, which we will get to. For a detailed video look at the HOR in action on the water, check out my website: www.garryhoyt.com

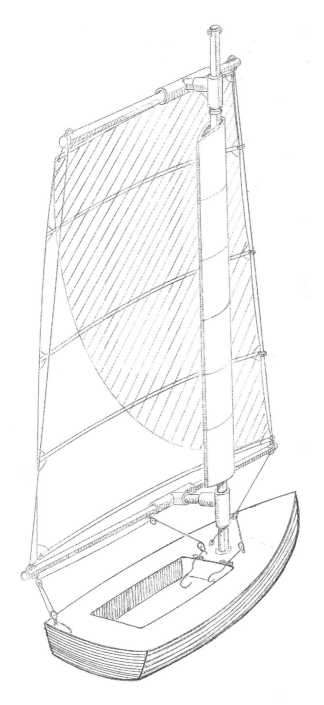

Hoyt Offset Rig

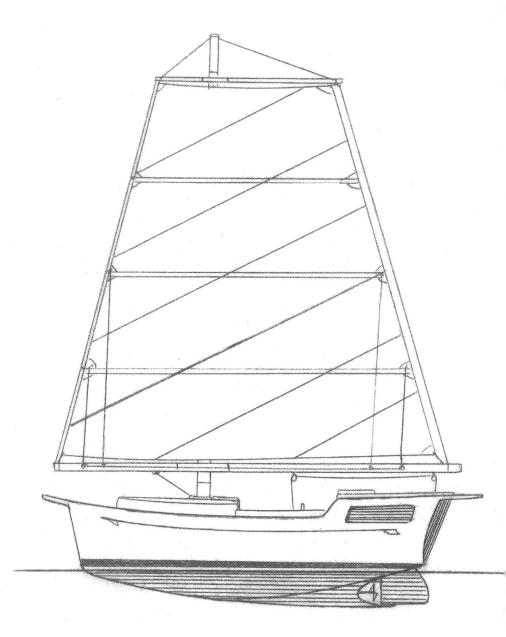

A balanced seagoing Cat Boat with Hoyt Offset Rig

Hoyt Offset Rig

Hoyt Offset Rig with Spinnaker

Hoyt Offset Rig

Hoyt Offset Rig

Hoyt Offset Rig

Hoyt Offset Rig

Chapter 3—The Nantucket Bay Skimmer

Now let's see how this unique combination of balanced, single sail, square head sail and clean leading edge might work on the classic American Catboat. Cat boats were the original American work boat, widely employed in Colonial America on the New England coast, where their shoal draft allowed them to fish and carry passengers in the many shallow bays and rivers in the area. I grew up sailing a Barnegat bay Sneakbox and still race a Marshall Cat on Nantucket, so I am very familiar with the virtues and vices of the genre.

In this design I have deliberately kept the unique Catboat configuration of high bow, bold sheer, shoal draft with centerboard and broad beam for stability and ample cockpit space with the mast set well forward. What I have eliminated with the balanced HOR rig is the horrendous weather helm and terrifying jibes that traditionally penalize Catboats. The permanent gaff aloft simplifies hoisting and lowering sail and the clean leading edge, hanked on to the wire forestay, will markedly improve windward performance. The HOR also enables quick reefing underway, which is not possible with the traditional gaff rig. I know all these features work because I have sailed the HOR on a 20 ft. day sailer hull for two summers. You can see for yourself by checking out my website: www.garryhoyt.com

My point with this design is that we can keep the unique, traditional charm of the classic American Cat Boat hull, powered by the compelling simplicity of the single sail rig. And by judicious rearrangement, we can put the gaff to better aerodynamic use in the horizontal mode. I can guarantee that this rig will be swifter, safer and simpler than the conventional Catboat. It is to be expected that this idea will be resisted by hide bound traditionalists who fail to see that often the best way to preserve tradition is by sensible refinement, rather than dogmatic insistence on preserving features that are neither swift, nor safe, nor simple.

I rest my case with the accompanying sketch showing a conventional Catboat broad reaching against a Nantucket Bay Skimmer. On the conventional Cat, the boom hikes wildly up and the gaff twists wildly off, making it impossible to effectively trim the sail, and inducing excessive weather helm that can make the boat uncontrollable. On the Nantucket Bay Skimmer with the balanced HOR, the boom is safely vanged, with the boom and gaff acting in concert to deliver full sail power with minimum weather helm. It's no contest, the HOR is swifter, safer and simpler. You can easily reef underway in seconds with single line reefing, and sail can be quickly hoisted and lowered without worrying about having the gaff come crashing down on your head. And best of all, we have preserved the shoal draft ability that first endeared Catboats to colonial America.

Nantucket Bay Skimmer

Nantucket Bay Skimmer

Chapter 4—The Quadrilateral Staysail Rig

This rig is an attempt to take advantage of the established acceptance and well proven gear for furling jibs, but incorporating them within the convenience of single sail control and the efficiency of an overall square headed profile. The drawings show how this could work with a simple three sail configuration. The specific advantages of this rig could be summarized as:

1. The ability to quickly unfurl, furl and reef all sails within sixty seconds without the bother of hoisting, lowering and messing with sail covers.

2. The efficiency of three clean leading sail edges with additional benefits from automatic slot effects, all controlled by a single sheet to a single main boom, linked to operate in concert with the gaff.

3. The ability to quickly achieve balanced sail reduction by simply furling up the #2 topsail.

4. The balance feature reduces sheeting loads and insures easy self tacking and stress free jibes.

So, in effect this rig is a single sail divided into three easily managed segments. I can see no reason why it should not be a very fast rig, ready to go or put away in an instant. For those greedy for more downwind speed, a carbon sprit can be housed in the forward end of the main boom, to extend out for more sail area.

The quadrilateral rig lets you control
3 furling sails with one balanced mainsheet.

Quadrilateral Rig

Garry Hoyt

Quadrilateral Rig

Chapter 5—The Caravel

This is a different application of the HOR, based on my twenty five years in the Caribbean, and close acquaintance with the charter scene there. In my view, the trouble with conventional chartering is not with the unsurpassed beauty of the Caribbean, nor with the unquestioned fact that chartering your own yacht may be the best way to savor it. The problem begins with the flawed notion that people should undertake this vacation adventure relentlessly compressed for seven days in the close company of one or two other couples in a thirty-six or forty-foot box! This is the kind of test that normal friendships are not designed to withstand. The first sacrifices are those moments of elementary privacy that everyone craves. Thence follows a series of pre-ordained stress points over who gets to steer, when and where to go, how best to anchor, who does the dishes, why does Mabel monopolize the head, and so on. Economy is the commonly touted rationale for this uncommonly uncivilized arrangement. But ask yourself, would you ever conceive of planning a vacation based on the bizarre compromise of sharing a hotel room anywhere, with two other couples, regardless of the savings involved? I think not.

A better way might start with the premise that your privacy is a fundamental right that deserves protection. So I've designed a special 32 ft. boat just for your and your chosen mate. It's called the Caravel—it's unabashedly romantic and serenely simple to sail. The single sail unfurls, reefs and furls away in seconds, all by solar powered electricity.

Caravels, you may recall, were the craft in which Columbus sailed the ocean blue and there are deliberately preserved traces of those historic lines in this hull design. But be not deceived by old fashioned looks. In rig, layout, construction and underbody, this is a very modern and efficient sailboat, easily able to hold her own with similar sized cruisers. And where this Caravel really trounces them is in single handed ease, stable comfort and *princely privacy.* By dividing the boat into three separate areas, we gain an appealing diversity of places to sit, read and relax, all in a very manageable size. Experienced sailors will note a master cabin with ventilation from four sides, plus three way views. Better than most fifty footers and with easy access to the water, so you can rise from your pad and dive overboard for a wake up swim if you like!

I have deliberately avoided deep fin keels and rudders, since deep draft prohibits sidling up close to the beaches. There is a small sacrifice in windward performance, but I assure you that if you just switch on your silent solar electric motor, you will glide right by the fastest racers, to their chagrin, because they won't be able to figure out your speed! And downwind the Caravel will trounce all of them, while you sail calmly by with rum drink in hand. I have shown a centerboard option that would make the Caravel fully competitive to windward as well.

In terms of prospects, one obvious invitation is to honeymooners, who certainly don't need company. Beyond that, there are many other sailors who would prefer to captain their own ship without having to cater to the perverse whims of others. Sure, it's nice to be with friends, let them charter their own Caravel, sail in company, raft up and be as chummy as you like. But you will always have your own ship and your own quiet space to retreat to. Older parents with grown kids may also appreciate this arrangement, which allows a family to be together—but not 24 hours a day. Note also that the rear projecting boomkin is a convenient base for safely carrying the dinghy aboard, rather than dragging it astern, where it is dangerously poised to bang your stern or foul your prop every time you slow or stop.

I have come around to accepting the reverse transom because of its practicality as a platform for easy swimming access to the water, similar ease in facilitating dinghy boarding and most important, as a permanent way back aboard for any man overboard emergency.

Caravel

Chapter 6—Multihull Applications of HOR

I suspect that the HOR may stand its best chance for early acceptance in the ranks of multihull sailors who tend to be less hung up on tradition and more prone to experimentation. They pay less attention to the orchestrated establishment objections and more attention to the added potential for speed and ease.

The adjoining sketches show 2 basic approaches, each with its share of advantages.

1. The Trimaran with Single Balanced Sail should develop tremendous sail power, yet could be quickly reefed down to a very small sail that is very easily handled.

2. The Catamaran with a single sail in each hull would deliver large sail area with a very low center of effort. Structurally this rig would significantly reduce the loads on the connecting center beam when the mast is in the center.

The width of multihulls also offers a natural opportunity for the wide exposure of solar panel cells, and the more easily driven narrow hulls can be powered by small electric auxiliary engines.

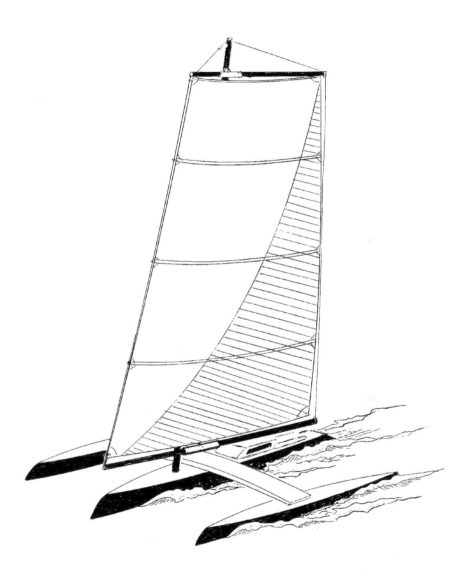

Hoyt Offset Rig On Trimaran

Trimaran with twin Hoyt Offset sails

Hoyt Offset Rig On Catamaran

Chapter 7—The Hoyt Jib Boom (HJB)

This patented invention, now in use on over 2000 boats, sprang directly from my frustration with the afore cited complications of the genoa jib. As a former Finn and Sunfish sailor, I maintained a lasting affection for single handed sailing, but since age deprived me of the hiking ability necessary to properly sail those dinghies, I moved to the greater security of a keel boat—namely the Alerion Express 28. This is a wonderful boat, skillfully designed by the late Carl Schumacher. This AE 28 was a beauty to see and sail and with a small self tacking jib it was a cinch to single hand. The only problem was the performance of the jib offwind. As the jib was eased, the leech would immediately twist away most of its power, leading to dismaying slowness. I tried going with a larger genoa, but that merely introduced the whole series of defects previously cited and crippled single handed ease.

As a designer and racer, it was clear to me that just as the main needs a vang to properly perform offwind, so too does the jib. The hard core racers compensate for the jib's offwind incapacity by just lowering the jib and hoisting a spinnaker, but that is a crew intensive procedure that is a contradiction of the vital single handed ease and pleasure. So what to do? Surely there had to be some way to make the jib perform offwind.

As described in an earlier chapter, I had already developed a free standing, self vanging mainsail boom for the Expo Solar Sailer. So I reasoned, why not utilize that same proven idea to create a self tacking, self vanging jib boom? Voila, a simple solution and it worked!

Since I was involved at the time as part of the design team at TPI (then the builder of the AE-28) I was able to promptly introduce the Hoyt Jib Boom as optional equipment on the Alerion Express 28. Experienced sailors were quick to see the performance benefit, and the HJB became a sales feature on all the new Alerions, as well as on all Island Packets and Harbor 20's. Beyond that, respected experts in the field provided candid and non paid endorsements, as evidenced by the following quotes.

Bengt Jornstedt—Editor—Segling—Leading Swedish Sailing Magazine

"I have used the Hoyt Jib Boom for three seasons on my 38 footer and I love it. It makes the headsail supremely easy to handle, giving full control at all times. To me, the most outstanding feature is its 'kick effect' ensuring efficient sail even when one starts to ease the sheet. Never again that hopelessly twisted leech—it's like having an invisible sheeting point out on the water. A marvel! I consider the Hoyt Jib Boom to be by far the best idea that has come out in many, many years."

Andrew Bray—Editor—Yachting World—Leading English Sailing Magazine

"When my boat, a 43 ft. wood/epoxy fast cruiser, was being built I wanted to have a furling self-tacking jib but was trying to solve the problem of changing the sheeting angle as the sail was reefed. One of my readers suggested the Hoyt Jib Boom.

I got far more than I bargained for. My sailmaker recognized the potential of the system and cut a sail with vertical full battens and a big roach. This develops enormous power on a reach as the Hoyt Jib Boom acts like a vang so I'm getting 100% of the horsepower from the sail and regularly outsail boats many feet longer. As for tacking, my crew complain that they are redundant as all they have to do is to change sides."

Bob Johnson—President/CEO—Island Packet Yachts

"Since the late 70's, the Island Packet range of sailboat models have been available with some form of staysail installation. These systems have evolved covering virtually every possible configuration from a simple loose footed flying staysail to club footed, roller furled systems on permanent stays. A Hoyt® boom was first incorporated for our staysail starting with the introduction of the Island Packet 350 about 6 years ago. We have used this configuration on every new Island Packet model since. The self-vanging aspect of the Hoyt® boom maintains excellent sail shape on all points resulting in considerably more drive from the staysail. A simple bridle sheet arrangement leads aft to the cockpit along with the roller furling line, so setting/furling or trimming the staysail is always convenient. Hundreds of Island Packets with these Hoyt® boom staysail rigs have now logged countless miles cruising worldwide in all varieties of conditions. I'd be hard pressed to improve on any aspect of this setup and would heartily recommend it to all cruising sailors."

Ken Read—America's Cup Helmsman, V.P. of North Sails and Volvo 70 Skipper

"The Hoyt Jib Boom is one of the best cruising innovations I have seen or used."

The Patented Hoyt Jib Boom (U.S. Pat.# 5,463,969) received *Sail Magazines'* 2000 Award for "Rigging Innovation of the Year".

It would be an exaggeration to say that the HJB has taken the market by storm—no such luck for the inventor! But it would be honest to report that everybody who or has used the HJB can see the benefits. Given the normally glacial pace of sailing's acceptance of new ideas—progress has been steady. Forespar now offers an attractive retro-fit package and little by little, people will come around. The HJB is still not attractive to hard core racers because its biggest speed advantage comes when reaching—and reaching courses have effectively been excised from the racing scene (a separate lapse of sanity) in favor of dogmatic attachment to the windward/leeward course. What sense does it make to eliminate the fastest and safest point of sail—which is the reach? Those who claim that reaches are a boring parade are really just confessing their skill limitations. The reach is where your boat should most come alive and the HJB can be instrumental in that.

By way of useful enhancements, the Harbor 20 introduced a simple system for curing the HJB's tendency to drift back to the centerline in light air. And the Alerions developed a system of pressurized pistons to address the same problem. Here is a summary of what the HJB does:

<u>What the HJB Is</u>: A free standing, self supporting, self vanging jib boom, swivelly mounted on the foredeck.

<u>What the HJB Does</u>:

1. *Automatically vangs the jib.* No serious sailor would sail without a mainsail boom vang. Yet up until now, they have been obliged to sail with unvanged jibs that twist off and lose power offwind. The Hoyt Boom holds the jib clew down, thus providing the firm leech control that keeps the entire sail drawing, on all courses.

2. *Acts as a built in whisker pole.* Downwind, conventional jibs just flop around and make a nuisance of themselves, resulting in a subtraction of sail power just when your boat needs more sail power. A whisker pole will solve this, but setting the pole requires work on the foredeck and every time you want to jibe, the foredeck work must be repeated. The Hoyt Jib Boom is poled out and jibed automatically by the wind—no foredeck work is involved.

3. *Allows Jib furling & reefing.* Being separate from the jib stay allows the convenience of roller furling and roller reefing. Being self supporting obviates any need for a topping lift. This boom holds itself up, while holding the clew down.

4. *Allows self tacking and 2:1 or 3:1 trim power.* Because a block or blocks can be carried at the end of the boom, jib trimming effort is significantly reduced, and in most cases can be accomplished with one hand—with no need for winching. The jib boom

self tacks with no trim required, which is a real boon for single handed sailing.

5. *The boom allows jib camber control independent of trim_angle.* With the conventional jib any easing of the sheet results in changing the angle as well as the camber of the sail. It is often desirable to change the camber of the sail to fuller or flatter, independent of the trim angle, and this HJB permits that.

How is this invention different from "regular" jib booms? Regular jib booms can be found on many older boats, but they never provided clew control and would dangerously hike up and lose power offwind (like a main boom without a vang.) They were known as "club" booms possibly because of the random facility with which they would "club" anyone venturing to the foredeck downwind.

Around the Buoys

Tests with the Alerions in winds over 12 knots have proven that a small jib with the Hoyt Jib Boom will out perform genoas around a triangular course. Because a small jib that works full time on all courses will beat a large, overlapping jib that only works upwind. Once you've tried it you'll wonder why everyone doesn't have one.

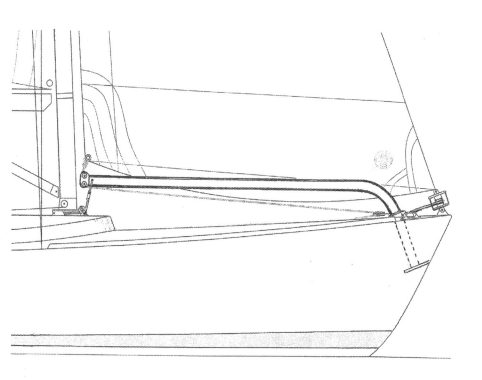

Hoyt Jib Boom
U.S. Patent No. 5,463,969

The Hoyt Jib Boom
vangs the jib and creates
an automatic whisker pole
that needs no foredeck work

Chapter 8—The Balanced Hoyt Jib Boom (BHJB)— (Patent Pending)

My experiments with various rigs have made me a firm advocate of the benefits of balance to lessen loads. A common example is the balanced rudder, which is virtually standard on all modern yachts for the simple reason that it makes steering significantly easier. Basically, the idea is to place the pivot point of the rudder about 20% back from the leading edge of the blade. (or the rig.) Thus, the oncoming flow reduces the effort needed to angle the controlling 80% of the blade. This advantage of balance, which is also employed in my offset rig, led me to seek a balanced version of the HJB.

In the conventional version of the HJB, the vertical leg of the boom, which is the pivot point, is located <u>behind</u> the deck attachment of the jib stay. The heart of the concept is that the angle of this vertical leg must match the angle of the forestay. That is essential in order to maintain constant leech tension as the sail is eased out, which is the purpose of the invention. This arrangement works fine, and is time tested in a variety of boats and weather conditions.

But what if we could lead the forestay down through the vertical leg, giving the jib one center of rotation instead of two? And once we have that, why not extend the HJB forward of the center of rotation? This would gain us the benefits of balance to lessen the sheeting loads like a balanced rudder. And most important, it would increase the potential size of the jib, which we know is the most effective sail—while still retaining the ease of self tacking. Sketching this out revealed we could gain a self tacking, self vanging jib that was almost as big in area as the genoa—and much bigger in effectiveness because it would not lose power when eased out—as the genoa inevitably does. And the forward extension of the jib automatically projects out to windward as the sheet is eased offwind—reducing weather helm.

At this point my mind's eye raced ahead, which it often alarmingly does. What if we could give this self tacking, self vanging, semi balanced, genoa sized jib the proven benefits of the square headed profile? Well why not? Why should we penalize this newly empowered jib with the handicap of the triangular shape, which we know is "the worst shape the aerodynamicist could invent?"

Then, in a blinding flash of the obvious, I saw a way to adapt the horizontal gaff developed for the Hoyt Offset Rig. By placing the forward projecting, light carbon, rotating gaff <u>on top of the</u> <u>mast</u>—instead of offset to the side as shown for the HOR—we could gain the necessary upper support for a square headed jib, thereby multiplying the jib's inherent clean leading edge advantage. (See drawing.) Now this would truly constitute an embarrassment of riches. Forgive the hyperbole, but a square headed, self tacking, self vanging, semi-balanced, fully battened genoa size jib would have to be a better performer. "But wait,"—as they say on TV—"There's more." Inside the forward projection of the deck mounted balanced Hoyt Jib Boom, we could house a retracting carbon sprit, which when extended would carry the tack of a large offwind staysail, giving us sail area equivalent to a large asymmetrical spinnaker. *With the significant advantage that all the sail trim angle would be controlled by the single existing jib sheet to the BHJB, which would be very lightly loaded due to the balance factor.* And the jibe would be a piece of cake instead of a major trauma. Whew!

And let the record show that this entire exercise in inventiveness (Patent Pending) has been conducted by my mind's eye plus pencil and paper—with no dependence on the computer! Take a look at the following sketches that show the BHJB in action.

Balanced Hoyt Jib Boom with Square Top Jib and Spinnaker

Balanced Hoyt Jib Boom with Square Top Jib

Balanced Hoyt Jib Boom with Square Top Jib on Schooner Rig

Balanced Hoyt Jib Boom with Spinnaker

Square Head Sail Schooner with
Balanced Hoyt Jib Boom and Spinnaker

Chapter 9—Solar Electric Power
As The Natural Ally Of Wind Power

In the first place, sun power is what creates wind power, so the pairing of the two is entirely natural. "The sun is the most abundant source of energy, delivering more energy to the earth in an hour than humanity uses in a year." *(NYTimes)* So that is a powerful, free source of energy ready to be tapped. And the use of solar electric power offers a clean, quiet propulsion that is fully compatible with the aesthetic appeal of sailing. Beyond that, solar power could open up an entirely new and attractive aspect of power boating. So rather than cursing recreational power boats for their current undeniable and undesirable contributions to noise, wakes and pollution, or simply trying to legislate them off the water, a better approach is to coax them into more sensible environmental ways. This should not be as hard as it might seem. For example, I do not believe that powerboaters have any innate love for the din, the clamor of engine noise that can make conversation impossible underway. They have simply accepted, along with the rest of us, that engine noise is the unavoidable price one has to pay for the ease and power of engine performance. But solar electric power offers another, better channel to the operating convenience that attracts most powerboaters, and solar power will add, rather than subtract—the benefits of silence and non pollution.

Of course electric power for cars has been explored and talked about in Detroit for years, and there is now hope that the press of new economic circumstances may yet peel the carbon scales from their eyes. The point here is that solar/electric is an alternative with advantages particularly suited to the recreational marine field, so its introduction there can be quicker and help show the way to the much larger field of land transportation. Be prepared for the onslaught of predictable objections. Critics will point out—correctly—that there currently is no proven electric engine ideally suited for marine use and that solar panels at present cannot deliver enough power. That is a logical reason to accelerate the necessary research and development. It is not a logical reason to disqualify or discourage this attractive alternative. One is reminded of the chorus of quavering voices that greeted John F. Kennedy's call for the U.S. to reach—and return from—the moon. The critics pointed out—correctly—that there were no engines at the time capable of generating the necessary thrust. Nor were there the navigational instruments capable of getting humans to the moon—to say nothing of getting them back. Nor were their metals capable of withstanding the intense heat generated by the friction of re-entry speeds. The list of impossibilities went on and on, and the fact that human ingenuity successfully solved them—in about a 10 year period—remains a feat that staggers the imagination. Alongside that achievement, building better solar panels, better batteries and better electric motors is relatively simple and completely doable. In fact a number of reputable companies have already developed working electric powered boats, so a lot of the start up work is done. What is most needed are improvements in the solar panels' collecting power, and in the batteries' storage power and durability.

And consider the special factors in favor of solar electric power for boats:

1. Batteries to store electric power are an essential ingredient of solar power and the burden of battery weight is significantly lessened by flotation. So a boat can comfortably carry the heavy battery weight that would cripple a car's mileage efficiency.

2. The use pattern of recreational boats—heavy on weekends and holidays—light every time else—gives solar cells ample down

time to fully recharge. This is in marked contrast to daily car use, which necessitates the complication of re-charging stations, or numerous battery exchange stations. Solar powered boats can be free and independent collectors of their own—clean, quiet power in the convenience of their own dock, mooring or backyard.

3. In the case of auxiliary power for sailboats, the burden of battery weight can be productively harnessed for ballast purposes, a wonderfully practical double use.

4. Solar electric power boats will require and reward newly efficient, slender shapes that slip through the waves rather than bash their way over them. The benefits here are both aesthetic and practical. The typical large power boat has a broad hull with flat after sections, which requires huge engines to lift it onto a plane, involving high cost, high noise, high wakes and high pollution. And when they throttle back, these planing hulls become even more inefficient, dragging half the bay with them and often generating waves that are bigger than those created by planing. This is not the smart way forward, so power boat design needs new thought and new hull shapes.

What this means is that solar/electric recreational power boats will have a wonderful opportunity to show the way to clean, quiet, low wake propulsion, with direct benefit to the surrounding bays, lakes, rivers and harbors. In many ways, these new solar powered hulls will draw on classic sailboat shapes that are more easily driven and require less horsepower, and look infinitely better. The hope is that this will lead to more cordiality and less single finger salutes as sailors and solar electric powerboaters meet and learn to nurture the resource they both love.

It is predictable that the first reaction of the power boat lobby will be denial and defiance. Who can forget the 20 Tobacco executives who swore under oath in front of a Congressional Committee that they never knew smoking was addictive, while denying the link between smoking and cancer? This is where sailors, rowers and kayakers need to unite in a task of friendly persuasion, backed by the ever increasing evidence. We can start by asking ourselves,

"Who Surrendered Our Original Right To Restorative Peace and Quiet on the Water?"

Well we all did. With the same passivity that we once endured the discomfort of smoke filled rooms, planes and restaurants, we all stood idly by as an armada of high powered outboards, jet skis and cigarette type boats routinely assaulted the peace, quiet and calm water that were once one of the presumed privileges and prime benefits of water recreation. After all, the reasoning went, "it's a free country and powerboaters have as much right to be on the water as we do." Yes, but what alters all that "fairness" argument is the emergence of compelling evidence to the clear and present danger from the use of carbon based fuels. So now, just as smoking and second hand smoke were proven injurious to our personal health, so carbon based fuel has proven seriously damaging to our global health, and that revelation disqualifies any protestation of equal rights for carbon based powerboats. And simultaneously, just as we have come to resent smoking as an intrusion on our fundamental right to fresh air—so we are now empowered to newly aroused indignation over the loss of our original and fundamental right to flat wakes and blessed quiet on the water.

Let me cite a flagrant example. From my office near Narragansett Bay you can hear—from 5 miles away—the engine roar when some mental juvenile—armed with an excess of gold chains and an acute shortage of smarts—hurls his overpowered Cigarette type craft against every passing wavelet, shattering the silence and menacing everything in his path as he careens down the bay under marginal control at fifty knots. This is an unacceptable violation of human patience and nature's health, and needs to be condemned as such. So rather than some gentle remonstrances for more environmental awareness, *Go For The Green* is a clarion call for a shift away from the recreational marine use of carbon based fuel. Obviously, the land based use of carbon fuels is a much larger problem, but the recreational marine use of carbon is a smaller, more manageable initial target that should be able to claim a broad based support constituency of rowers, canoeists, kayakers and sailors. This group is the best place to start, because they have a natural preference that coincides with the national need. Of course any move of this nature will face organized outrage from powerboat magazines, powerboat builders, powerboat dealers and powerboat owners—a formidable aggregate with strong political clout. None of that alters the pervasive need for corrective action that will inevitably involve initial pain for eventual gain.

This does not mean we should get carried away with misguided missionary zeal. The task here is not the upwind battle to convert powerboaters to sail, but rather to join them in a quest for cleaner, quieter, more environmentally kind engines that can serve powerboaters as better primary power and can also serve sailboats as better auxiliary power.

Chapter10—The Solar Cell Sail As New Dual Purpose Power

The concept is simple. When the wind is with us, as in—behind us—let's go with the wind. And when the wind isn't, let's go with sun powered electric prop power. This calls for a special design that does what the wind makes easy—run before it—but doesn't try to do what the wind makes difficult—which is to go against it.

Accepting those parameters opens up interesting possibilities. First, not having to go to windward lets us get rid of tall rigs and deep keels and allows us a very clean underbody with shoal draft capacity. And for downwind efficiency, all we really need is to the barn door effect of ample sail area, so we could get rid of complex rigging and exotic sail cloth. And so why not go with a rigid carbon sail structure that could be surfaced with power producing solar panels? And while we're about it, let's make this rigid sail capable of folding up to the vertical to maximize wind collecting power and folding down to the horizontal to maximize solar collecting capacity. The horizontal mode would also minimize wind resistance under power. And by dividing the rigid sail into three overlapping, folding panels, we could gain expandable sail and solar power, while retaining compact size.

Let's accept at the outset that this new craft is not likely to please either hard core sailors or diehard power boaters. Our aim here is to attract some new, non polluting middle ground. Actually the performance potential of this new craft will be quite surprising. For downwind sailing this Solar Sailer would be very fast due to large, effectively deployed sail area and clean underbody. The balanced nature of the rig would also make it supremely easy to steer, while completely de-fusing the dangers of the jibe. Upwind under solar prop power, the Solar Sailer will be able to go wherever you want to go in a straight line at hull speed. Thus in net speed to windward it would be significantly faster than similar sized conventional sail craft, with no noise, no heeling and no fuel cost. Add in the attraction of a yacht that could recharge its batteries at anchor and possibly also draw charging power from the rotation of the prop downwind. To the rational thinker, this is an imposing array of assets that might create a new category of boating pleasure.

Think for a moments how this Solar Sailer could neatly address the habitual (and valid) objections of power boaters to sailboats—namely that sailboats are:

1. Too slow

2. Too complex

3. Too tippy

4. Too crew intensive

5. Too unable to go in a straight line where you want to go

6. Too unable to handle shallow water

7. Too dependent on wind velocity

8. Too prone to catching pots and nets on the deep keel

And for the casual, coastal cruiser, imagine how pleasant it would be to have the convenience of power without the noise, expense and gratuitous pollution of power, along with the cachet of being a sailor!

Fold Up Solar Cell Sail

Chapter 11—Reprise

Part II of *Go For The Green* has attempted to show some design solutions to improve sail power based on various combinations of 3 positive factors:

1. The Importance of the Sail's Clean Leading Edge

2. The Value of the Square Head Sail Profile

3. The Benefits of Sail Balance for Safety and Reduced Sheeting Loads

I make no claim to any particular originality in any of the above, although I have tried to explore some new possibilities. And of course candor compels me to point out that the actual speed results gained by any of the above—are relatively minor. But then progress in sail power has always consisted of marginal, incremental, minor refinements to a very modest speed base. And it is in this cultivation of subtle refinements that much of sailing's appeal lies. The accomplished sailor is forever fiddling with minor adjustments in order to coax his craft into better harmony with wind and waves. And it is the awareness of, and appreciation for the constant interaction between wind angle, sail angle, wave angle, rudder angle and heeling angle that makes sailing skill as satisfying to the sailor as it is mystifying to the non sailor. My modest hope is to have added some new ingredients for your consideration.

What is perhaps immodest is my impertinence in calling for a sea change in our heretofore passive acceptance of petroleum based power for recreational boating. To larger sight, that acceptance is just not good enough, and –as cited earlier—is closely akin to society's long standing tolerance and cinematic celebration of cigarette smoking, despite the steady accumulation of damaging evidence. At the risk of preaching I believe that in the collective public mind, petroleum needs to be deposed from its present preeminence as our primary source of power, and be more accurately re-classified as a dirty old fuel that has dangerously overplayed its hand to the direct detriment of our global health. And by way of useful side effects, removing the prop of our misplaced petroleum affection will force a number of repressive regimes and tin horn dictators back into their proper insignificance.

But for this to happen, it is not enough to just join the now fashionable chorus for alternative fuels like sun, wind and nuclear. Of course those alternatives must be put into place as soon as possible. But to make room for them to survive and grow, petroleum must first be actively displaced as the favorite in the public mind. This is an enormous challenge, the sheer scope of which is enough to discourage its adoption. Who amongst us is willing to give up the petroleum based conveniences which we have all grown up with as part of what we perceive to be the good life?

This is where I see a very small but potentially significant role for sailors, rowers, kayakers and canoeists, because they may be the only group in America who have voluntarily—and enthusiastically—already done what we must do nationally—which is to give up petroleum based propulsion for other more natural means. Granted, the numbers of sailors, rowers, etc. are numerically insignificant, as indeed is the whole field of marine recreation. But do not underestimate the ability of a small spear head group to interrupt the present petroleum power boat paradigm. Sailors in particular can begin to insist on solar electric auxiliary engines as the logical, natural sequitur to sail power. The fact that sailboat auxiliary engine use is an exceedingly minor source of pollution is not beside the point—it is the point, because somebody has to lead this parade—and the case needs to be made on the strength of environmental principle over the convenience of current habits.

So let's come clean, go green, lose the carbon, and find our way back to the freedom and silent splendor of the sea. We owe it to our grandchildren and to the noble exploratory traditions of sail—the most ancient medium of discovery and the most modern way to responsibly savor the sea.

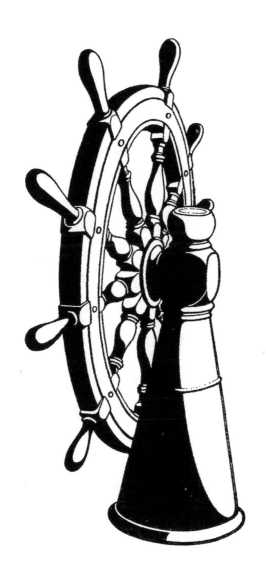

ABOUT THE AUTHOR . . . . . .

Garry Hoyt was the 1970 World Champion Sunfish sailor, who has sailed in the Olympics and won numerous regional One Design Championships on the U.S. East Coast and in the Caribbean. As the founder of Freedom Yachts, he pioneered the development of the freestanding spar for larger cruising yachts, beginning with the Freedom 40, a design that won a variety of cruising titles in the Caribbean. Hoyt's production designs include the Freedom 21, 25, 29, 32, and 44. He collaborated with the Harkens in the design of modern pedal powered boats—the Waterbug and the Mallard and he later designed the Escape line of roto-molded small sailboats. In January 2000 he was named by *Sail Magazine* as one of the most influential sailors in the past thirty years, and his patented Hoyt Jib Boom received *Sail Magazine's* award for innovation of the year. In 2001 he received *Sail's* award for Industry Leadership for contributions to the sport.

As a writer, Hoyt has authored three books, *Go For The Gold, Ready About,* and *Isla Verde,* as well as numerous articles for sailing magazines. In his earlier career in advertising, he worked for *Young and Rubicam,* including twenty five years in San Juan, Puerto Rico where his two sons were born. During that period he traveled extensively to Latin America, the Far East and regional offices in the U.S. as an area manager. In 1980 moved back to the U.S. and took up a career in boat design. He met and married his wife Donna in 1982 and they currently reside in Newport, RI. He remains an active sailor and on Nantucket in 2006 was the overall winner of the *Opera House Cup* in an Alerion 26—the smallest boat in the fleet.

A 1952 graduate of *Colgate University,* where he majored in English literature, Hoyt also received a graduate degree from the *Thunderbird School of International Management.* He served as a Lieutenant J.G. in the *U.S. Coast Guard* with search and rescue duties in Florida and the Caribbean.